Taking Jesus
To Work

"The Great Commission is being carried out every day in a myriad of work settings by people from all walks of life. Yet the importance of this 'ministry work' often goes unnoticed by the Body of Christ. *Taking Jesus to Work* brings marketplace evangelism front and center and offers a practical tool for effectiveness."

—**Bishop T. D. Jakes Sr.**

"I have long said that we need authentic men and women of God to be salt and light in the marketplace. The Body of Christ desperately needs an army of courageous men and women who will make marketplace evangelism a mandate. As we begin to take the Gospel to the places where we earn a living, we will experience revival in our nation. *Taking Jesus to Work* will mobilize us for this action."

—**Bishop Wellington Boone**,
Fellowship of International Churches

"*Taking Jesus to Work* is a must-read for those who understand that the harvest is ripe right where they are planted, regardless of the environment in which they find themselves. It provides sound wisdom, practical tools and biblical principles to share one's faith effectively in the real world of work!"

—**Patricia R. Johnson**, Ph.D., J.D.

"This book is a pastor's dream: a profound yet practical manual for every believer to turn his or her workplace into a harvest field for souls while pursuing a successful career. Everywhere I have gone, I have seen the desperate need for the integrity and truth to which Dr. Vera is so passionately committed, and which is evident on every page of this book. If every Christian followed the principles outlined in *Taking Jesus to Work*, we would soon see our culture transformed for the glory of God."

—from the foreword by **Bishop Harry R. Jackson Jr.**, senior pastor,
Hope Christian Church

"As an entrepreneur committed to biblical principles, I am very encouraged to see Jackson's book spell out so precisely and comprehensively how we can apply the teachings of our faith in the marketplace. The stories she shares challenge and edify believers of all walks of life."

"*Taking Jesus to Work* serves as a road map for finding and succeeding at your marketplace assignment while developing character, integrity and a closer relationship with Jesus Christ. When I read the book, I thought about the things God had spoken to me in times past about marketplace evangelism. I meditated on the principles in the book and prayed the prayers in each chapter. As I did, I asked God to open a door for me so that I could leave semi-retirement and return to full-time work. Soon thereafter, God used a former co-worker to tell me about a position. I applied for the position and received it! Now with a renewed focus, I have returned to the marketplace to be God's beacon of light in dark places and a guide for those who need Jesus."

"Vera Jackson's book offers one of the most compelling and challenging discussions of marketplace ministry that I have ever encountered. If every Christian would apply what she outlines, we would soon see our world transformed."

"This book emphasizes the call for consistent righteous living. Mrs. Jackson introduces witnessing techniques that can be used in and out of the workplace."

"This book inspires and encourages the reader to view ministry beyond the four walls of the church and in the heart of the marketplace."

Taking Jesus To Work

*Learning To Release Strong Faith
In The Workplace*

Dr. Vera R. Jackson

Kingdom Living Publishing
Accokeek, MD

Unless otherwise indicated, Scripture is taken from the HOLY BIBLE, NEW INTERNATIONAL VERSION®. NIV®. Copyright © 1973, 1978, 1984 by International Bible Society. Used by permission of Zondervan. All rights reserved.

Scripture marked AMP is taken from the Amplified ® Bible, Copyright © 1954, 1958, 1962, 1964, 1965, 1987 by The Lockman Foundation. Used by permission.

Scripture marked ASV is taken from the *American Standard Version* of the Bible.

Scripture marked NKJV is taken from the New King James Version of the Bible. Copyright © 1982 by Thomas Nelson, Inc. Used by permission. All rights reserved.

Scripture marked KJV is taken from the King James Version of the Bible.

Note: Some names and details have been changed throughout this book to protect those whose stories appear here.

Published by:

Kingdom Living Publishing
P.O. Box 660
Accokeek, MD 20607
www.kingdomlivingbooks.com

ISBN 978-0-615-54055-9

Printed in the United States of America

This book is dedicated
in loving memory of my parents,
Jesse and Ruth Royster.

Acknowledgments

With love, gratitude, adoration and praise, I thank God for trusting me with His Kingdom work in the marketplace and for allowing me the expression of these experiences.

To my husband, Wilbert, and children, Brandon and Anjelica, thank you for your loving support that has enabled me to pursue this and other dreams.

To my brother, Ronn, thank you for speaking words to me that have lifted and inspired.

To my dearest friends, thank you for your prayers and words of encouragement.

Lastly, thanks so much to Irma McKnight for helping me to complete this third edition.

Contents

Foreword

We all know people who feel torn between their jobs and their service for the Kingdom of God. Ironically, many well-meaning mentors push blossoming believers to make premature and often permanent choices about their careers and their futures. When I was in my twenties, I was encouraged to enter full-time ministry too early. As a result of a poorly timed and even more poorly implemented decision to "live by faith," I put my family through unnecessary years of financial sacrifice and loss of focus. In my own case, I exalted the idea of "full-time" ministry far beyond its important role. In some ways, I saw full-time service as God's highest calling—instead of one of His many callings.

As senior pastor of a multiracial church, I have often lamented that many Christians seem to separate their "ministries" from their careers. Too often they believe they must wait to be ordained or enter full-time vocational ministry before preaching the Gospel and winning the lost. How much easier my job, and those of so many like me, would be if all believers understood that they were sent by God to proclaim the Gospel everywhere—even at their places of employment.

I have also seen believers minimize the importance of non-staff volunteer roles like leadership, teaching, worship, leading or administration. If you are someone who wants to find your own niche and truly understand marketplace ministry, this book may be a word from God for you.

In the years that I have known and mentored Dr. Vera Jackson, she has exemplified that understanding. Our church has always sought to equip members to minister wherever they go, and Dr. Vera has been a vital part of those efforts. In addition to her business and leadership acumen, her lifestyle and testimony serve as wonderful examples of how to live and work for Jesus.

Despite her professional accomplishments, Dr. Vera has served with enthusiasm, integrity and humility wherever I have needed her. From highly visible roles to much less glamorous tasks, Dr. Vera's work ethic and faithfulness have exemplified the character of Jesus. In all this, I have seen her keep her husband and her children as her top priority.

This book is a leader's dream: a profound yet practical manual for every believer to turn his or her workplace into a harvest field for souls while pursuing a successful career. It details the strategies you will need, as well as the challenges you will face. It offers a sound scriptural foundation for creative evangelism to strengthen and inspire your efforts along the way. It also encourages you as a marketplace Christian to respond to the Holy Spirit's guidance to become a creative, energetic and innovative witness for Jesus while at work.

As you read this book, you will discover:

- God's vision and priorities for Christians in the professional world

- How to free yourself from counterproductive attitudes and mindsets

- How to take advantage of unique ministry opportunities in the workplace
- How your excellence can become cultural influence
- How to advance professionally without compromising your faith

For the past several years I have traveled the nation and the world, speaking to the vital issues of our day. Everywhere I have gone, I have seen the desperate need for the integrity and truth to which Dr. Vera is so passionately committed, and which is evident on every page of this book. If every Christian followed the principles outlined in *Taking Jesus to Work*, we would soon see our culture transformed for the glory of God.

Bishop Harry R. Jackson Jr.
Senior Pastor, Hope Christian Church

1

Why Am I Here?

Have you ever reached over on a Monday morning to hit that snooze button one more time? I know I have. Maybe you had a really busy weekend and feel exhausted. Maybe you know that as soon as you arrive at the office, an overwhelming project will await your attention on your desk. We may all have days when we do not feel like getting up for work, but we should always know *why* we get up and go.

No matter what your position, industry or role at work, you are not at your current job by accident. You are there to do so much more than collect your paycheck and pay your bills. If you are a follower of Jesus Christ and God has blessed you with a job, He has handpicked you to be His salt and light in the marketplace.

A Light in the Darkness

For a period of time shortly after my entrance into the workforce, I could have been referred to as a "quick job-change artist." I was already a committed Christian at the time, yet I darted from one job to the next, holding four different jobs over three years. I stayed in one position less than nine months. Each time, I was the one who ended the assignment, feeling that I needed to "move on." I cited numerous reasons for my quick departures: My boss was mean; my co-workers were lazy or irresponsible; no one in the office seemed to take the company's mission seriously; and several co-workers were cheating on their spouses. My godly disgust with each of these situations seemed to make life unbearable, and soon enough I would give my notice and move on.

These quick job changes did not go unnoticed. Loved ones began to inquire about my employment instability. I quickly tired of their questions, and rather than share a detailed account of my experiences, I devised a one-size-fits-all explanation. "Darkness," I would respond stoically. "I left my job because I was surrounded by darkness." I was great at selling this rationale. Soon friends and family were shaking their heads sympathetically and agreeing that I had chosen the only acceptable option in every case. I was young and highly employable, yet the perfect job seemed perpetually out of reach.

Predictably, the abrupt starts and stops began to take a toll on me. Physically I seemed okay, but I began buckling under the weight of mental and emotional stress, and my spirit was far from peaceful. When I took the time to examine my feelings, I realized I felt unfulfilled and sad. *Here I am*, I thought, *trying to follow the Lord, taking a stand against darkness by leaving intolerable work environments—yet something is terribly wrong.*

One night, I cried out to God in sheer desperation. I knelt in prayer and asked, *Why do I feel this way, Lord? Why am I constantly confronted with darkness in the places where You have made it possible for me to work? Where is the light?*

Almost instantaneously, a still, small voice answered me in my spirit: *You are the light.*

That moment forever changed my entire outlook on work and my role in the marketplace. Suddenly, I understood that I carried the presence of God with me even in the darkest and most uncomfortable places where He had blessed me with the opportunity to work. This was the beginning of an ongoing revelation for me and laid the foundation for so much more that I would experience later.

> The marketplace is like a schoolroom God uses for our instruction in righteousness.

Mission Possible

As the Lord taught me more about this unique ministry of taking Jesus to work and living out my faith on the job, I began to understand that our assignment in the marketplace is to be a vessel for God's anointing. Amazingly, our function as God's vessels of light in the marketplace has a lot in common with the function of a vocational minister. In both cases, individuals need to be ready and willing for God to use them whenever and however He chooses. We cannot meditate on that truth long without realizing that fulfilling our marketplace assignment requires not only professional excellence but also an uncompromising devotion to God.

Consider the life of Joshua:

> *But if serving the Lord seems undesirable to you, then choose for yourselves this day whom you will serve, whether the gods your forefathers served beyond the River, or the gods of the Amorites, in whose land you are living. But as for me and my household, we will serve the Lord.*
>
> Joshua 24:15

God uses all of our experiences. He places us as "missionaries in the marketplace" not only so we can evangelize the lost, but also so He can shape us into His image while He uses us to touch unbelievers. The marketplace is like a schoolroom God uses for our instruction in righteousness. It is a place where character flaws, duplicity and double-mindedness are exposed so God can correct us and make our words and actions consistent with our beliefs.

Our marketplace assignment develops and perfects our personal testimonies of faith, commitment and trust in God. While at times this process can be painful, God deliberately and lovingly plants us in places where He can work out the imperfections in our lives. The temptation to leave in the middle of an assignment may be great, as it was for me early in my career. Yet while our flesh is attracted to comfortable outward conditions, God values our inner maturity too much to let us slide. This level of maturity is what Paul references in Ephesians 4:11–15:

It was he who gave some to be apostles, some to be prophets, some to be evangelists, and some to be pastors and teachers, to prepare God's people for works of service, so that the body of Christ may be built up until we all reach unity in the faith and in the knowledge of the Son of God and become mature, attaining to the whole measure of the fullness of Christ.

Then we will no longer be infants, tossed back and forth by the waves, and blown here and there by every wind of teaching and by the cunning and craftiness of men in their deceitful scheming. Instead, speaking the truth in love, we will in all things grow up into him who is the Head, that is, Christ.

Do not be surprised if you find people at work who are struggling with an area of weakness similar to something you have dealt with yourself. I have come to realize that we are meant to share liberally with others the growth lessons we learn from our marketplace assignments for their benefit and for the glory of God. As we take this task seriously, we will begin to experience genuine compassion for the people who are outside the protection of the Most High God. We will eagerly and wholeheartedly partner with God as He draws men and women to Himself.

> Work is a blessing and an assignment to expand God's Kingdom.

God's Plan for Work

Everyone might like the idea of taking a permanent vacation, but in reality work has been part of God's plan for mankind from the beginning.

The Lord God took the man and put him in the Garden of Eden to work it and take care of it. And the Lord God commanded the man, "You are free to eat from any tree in the garden."

Genesis 2:15–16

This interaction between God and the first man took place before sin entered the earth. The Lord has always intended for us to work and eat the fruit of our labors. Idleness has never been part of His will. In fact, "having nothing to do" is part of the fall of man.

We know that Jesus came to save us from sin and bring us into the Kingdom of God. In Matthew 20, He tells a parable that illustrates His call for us:

He agreed to pay them a denarius for the day and sent them into his vineyard. About the third hour he went out and saw others

21

standing in the marketplace doing nothing. He told them, "You also go and work in my vineyard, and I will pay you whatever is right." So they went.

Verses 2–5

God is calling us to labor in His vineyard. He wants to rescue us from idleness by calling us to work, and He has enough going on to keep all of us busy. Not only that, He has promised to reward us for our labor. It just does not get better than that!

It is easy to imagine that we are laboring in God's vineyard when we volunteer for our church or do other ministry work. Yet God intends that the marketplace jobs we do every day be set apart for His glory just as much as if we were pastoring a church or traveling as an evangelist. God wants us to see all the work we do as a holy calling. Paul said it this way: *"Whatever you do, work at it with all your heart, as working for the Lord, not for men"* (Colossians 3:23).

Work is a blessing. We all understand this when we are out of a job and need to find employment to keep the bills paid. Yet God's purpose for our work goes so far beyond meeting our financial needs. Each job or "assignment" we receive from Him is part of His divine plan to expand His Kingdom. Unfortunately, there are still people—and some believers are among them—who stand idle in the marketplace just like the men in the parable. Some are lazy, but others simply do not understand why they are there. They do not know God's plan for work.

God wants to make sure we are fulfilling the roles He prepared for us before we were born. The Bible teaches us that God judges us based on our stewardship of what He entrusts to us in this life. When it comes to our professional lives, we know He is interested in how we spend the money we earn and how we treat the people we meet. Do we also realize that He is just as interested in the quality of the work we do?

22

Passport to the Lost

Think about the lives of missionaries. They leave the comfort of their homeland to take the Gospel to people who would never have the chance to hear it otherwise. Missionaries know when they enter a new land that they may be the only representatives of Jesus Christ that the people ever see. They conduct themselves in a way that is above reproach to avoid hurting their Lord's reputation. In short, they live their lives on the mission field exactly the way we should live our lives when we go into the marketplace.

The most obvious meaning of the word *missionary* is "someone on a mission." That is who we are! First and foremost, our work in the marketplace is a passport that affords us entrance into the lives of lost people we would never otherwise meet. They may be struggling in their families, suffering from past hurts or simply searching for purpose and meaning in life. They are people made in the image of God, people whom He loves dearly.

> Our work in the marketplace is a passport that affords us entrance into the lives of people.

Think of it—you may be the only real Christian that the people on your job ever get to see. With every breath you take and every step you make, He is calling you to fulfill the Great Commission. Certainly our Sovereign God does not *need* our help, yet in His mercy He has chosen to use you and me. When we cooperate with God's plan for us to live out our faith on the job, our lives become enormously full, joyous and purposeful.

God is calling us to take the Gospel to those we supervise, to our co-workers and even to our superiors. That is what it means to be salt and light in the marketplace! Just as God sends missionaries overseas to bring the Gospel to other cultures, He sends each one of us to our unique professional subculture to carry His Good News. When men and women see us as loving and compassionate people who set a standard for excellence in all we do, they will be drawn to the God we serve.

In order for us to accomplish our mission, however, we must understand the importance of the positions we hold and the professional roles we play. We must understand that God will give us the wisdom and strength to please our earthly bosses and our heavenly Boss! We do not need to compromise one for the other. When we are focused on faithfully representing Jesus in our character, conduct and work ethic, we cannot help but perform on the job with excellence.

Prayers for Knowledge

Jesus sums up this divine combination of holiness and excellence in Matthew 10:16: *"I am sending you out like sheep among wolves. Therefore be as shrewd as snakes and as innocent as doves."* We must never think that being spiritual means being ignorant! Jesus tells us that it is possible to be wiser than the world and yet remain untainted by its ways. Throughout this book, we will see that prayer is the foundation for this godly wisdom. Here are seven specific points we will pray about and address in the chapters that follow:

1. **Pray for knowledge of the marketplace culture and its workers.** If you have the freedom, you might pick a day to arrive early to work or to stay late to prayer walk around the office. Be sure to pray through any thoughts God brings to your heart until you sense a release. You

might also read company publications like newsletters and annual reports to gain insight into any pressing concerns. You can then pray for those needs on a daily basis.

2. **Pray for knowledge to fulfill God's purpose in the marketplace.** Commit all your important workplace activities to prayer, especially the words you speak. Pause on a regular basis and prayerfully consider whether your words will edify or discourage, build up or tear down.

3. **Pray for knowledge to discern how you can effectively apply biblical principles to every situation you face.** As God increases your discernment, you will be able to express biblical truths confidently without depending on "religious" language.

4. **Pray for knowledge of the character of God. Remember, your time alone in God's Word is equipping you to be an effective employee.** Do not forget to continually identify aspects of God's character in His Word and meditate on them. You might even pray for an opportunity to demonstrate some aspect of these characteristics in your work. Always ask for God's favor to provide the best service or product you can, which alone will reflect the excellence of God.

5. **Pray for knowledge to evangelize and disciple others.** Pray that God would reveal the individuals He has assigned to you. Ask for His wisdom to know how to approach them. Do not become known for chastising them when they fail. Find creative ways to show them how to make better decisions. A co-worker once confided to me that she was engaged in an adulterous relationship. Rather than scold her for sinful behavior, I talked with her about what she was risking and what she could lose as a result of her choices. As we continued to talk, over

time God opened the door for me to share my faith with her and lead her to Christ.

6. **Pray for knowledge about how to please God first.** Pray that God will prevent you from being swayed by either the applause or the condemnation of men. Perform your work as if God were your boss—which He is!

7. **Pray for knowledge to remain holy.** Pray that God will protect you from the schemes of the enemy to pollute you with sin. Work with confidence in God's plan. Be receptive to the intercessors that God will send to be your prayer shield and support. Listen to their words, and then pray for further revelation regarding every issue or need.

To further emphasize the importance of this spiritual growth process of becoming God's salt and light in the marketplace, an "Equipping Prayer" is offered at the end of each chapter for you to use and expand on. A "Marketplace Memory Scripture" also highlights God's perspective and serves as a reminder that God's Word should be your standard. To wrap it all up, the "Marketplace Experience Self-Evaluation" helps you look at where you stand now in your mission to the marketplace and where you can go from here as God uses you to make a difference in your work world.

Can God Count on You?

God is seeking disciples whom He can use. God wants to bless you and use you for great things in the marketplace. But first, you must let go of yesterday's hurts and move full force with God into the future He has in store for you. It is easier than you think. Begin by believing that God has something very special in store for you at work. Before you know it, you will find your-self laboring in the Master's vineyard and receiving His good rewards.

Now that we understand that God has sent us to the market-place with a specific mission, we are ready to take a closer look at the typical challenges faced by believers in a new assignment or on a first job. In chapter 2, let's look at how we can avoid para-lyzing emotions such as fear and consider more closely our call to become righteously strategic in the workplace.

―――――――――*Equipping Prayer*―――――――――

Father, thank You for allowing us to search Your Word and be-come convinced of Your truth regarding our assignment to live out our faith on the job. Please give us what we need to be more effective in the places where You send us. Lord, please pour out Your Word in a fresh and new way. In the precious and mighty name of Jesus we pray, Amen.

―――――――― **Marketplace Memory Scripture** ――――――――

" 'If you can'?" said Jesus. "Everything is possible for him who believes."

Mark 9:23

Marketplace Experience Self-Evaluation

Take some time after reading each chapter to answer these self-evaluation questions in a notebook that can become your Marketplace Journal. Writing down your answers will help you look closely at where you stand now in your mission to the marketplace and where you can go from here.

Record a time when you did not understand God's plan for work or when you left your job before your assignment was up.

Based on the teaching in chapter 1, list one biblical principle you could have applied to your situation.

What are some ways that you demonstrate your faith in the workplace?

When was the last time you shared the Gospel with someone from work?

Based on the teaching in chapter 1, rate your new skill level at taking Jesus to work and living out your faith on the job:

    ___ 1.   A Little Better Prepared
    ___ 2.   Much Better Prepared
    ___ 3.   Equipped

Note: *To increase your skill level after your initial reading of this chapter, please pray for wisdom according to James 1:5: "If any of you lack wisdom, he should ask God, who gives generously to all without finding fault, and it will be given to him," and read the chapter again.*

2

Spying Out the Land

I said to you, "You have reached the hill country of the Amorites, which the Lord our God is giving us. See, the Lord your God has given you the land. Go up and take possession of it as the Lord, the God of your fathers, told you. Do not be afraid; do not be discouraged." Then all of you came to me and said, "Let us send men ahead to spy out the land for us and bring back a report about the route we are to take and the towns we will come to."

Deuteronomy 1:20–22

Moses spoke of courage to the Israelites who stood on the border of the Promised Land. After two generations of wandering in the desert, they stood on the brink of something entirely new. They were about to enter the territory the Lord had promised them, but first they had to spy out the land.

For a Kingdom representative in the marketplace, entering a new job or accepting a new position is often like standing on the brink of a new realm the Lord has promised you. You may feel the way the Israelites felt—a little excited and a little intimidated. Like them, you need to spy out the land before you take any drastic action. You need to take a good look at your surroundings, your boss, your co-workers and your subordinates. You need to analyze your environment and your job professionally and spiritually, and then with God's guidance determine the best strategy to fulfill His will for you in your new position. Spying out the land is part of God's preparation process for His representatives in the marketplace. It readies us to act as His "living epistles" who proclaim the Gospel of Jesus Christ at work.

Prayer Point: Pray for knowledge of the marketplace culture and its workers.

When Moses sent twelve spies into the Promised Land, only two came back with a report that matched the promises of God. The other ten told with trembling voices of the awesome stature of the giants who lived there and assured the Israelites that they had no chance to enter in. We still have such faithless spies in our midst today. How often have you been ready to accept that new position, ask your supervisor for a raise or go back

Heavenly Father, please help me to become more discerning of situations, assignments and people in the marketplace so that I will excel in sharing the Gospel. In Jesus' name I pray, Amen.

to school, but all you have heard from family and friends are negative reports?

"You'll never be able to do *that* job."

"There's no way you'll get a raise!"

"You? Go back to school? Why?"

The good news is that when God instructs you to spy out the land, He is not doing so to fill you with fear or discouragement. He wants to prepare you for His purposes in the marketplace.

Once you have spied out the land with His eyes, you can answer every naysayer with confidence.

Scoping Out the Territory

God has chosen you as one of His living epistles to the marketplace—you are a leader with a strategic mission. Your mission, if you choose to accept it, is to complete your assignment while faithfully representing the Lord to everyone you meet. As with any other mission, preparation is the key to long-term success. You need to know where you are being sent and whom you will encounter there. You need to gird yourself up for the professional tasks, the emotional challenges and the spiritual battles ahead.

Spying out the land in practical terms can mean many different things. You will probably need to talk to people who have worked at your new company for a while about their experiences. You need not be specific with your questions; just get to know the people and take mental notes about what it will be like to work there and what the general expectations are. Be sure to talk to a variety of people and take full advantage of company publications, as well as gathering outside information from books and news articles.

With God on our side, we can defeat every giant in the marketplace!

As you gather information, focus on how God is the final authority in your life. If what you learn is disturbing, remember that He will work all things together for your good, whether it looks possible in the natural or not. If your fact-finding mission causes you to burst with excitement, on the other hand, remember it is still likely that some trials lie ahead to build your character.

Early in my career, I received an appointment to work in a world-class city on a critical initiative impacting families. I had no clue what I was getting myself into. I was young and naïve. Confident in my educational credentials and sophisticated demeanor, I never bothered to spy out the land. To make matters worse, I never checked with God to find out if He wanted me to accept that assignment in the first place. It was a great opportunity professionally, so I assumed it was God's will.

I accepted the appointment with tremendous excitement and high hopes for the legacy I would leave in that city. What a rude awakening I received instead! I soon found myself in way over my head, involved in a bureaucratic mess that had been decades in the making. I tried to do my job despite the completely dysfunctional environment, but my recommendations fell on deaf ears and were useless. I became frustrated, discouraged and even depressed.

The corporate culture of that office made Sodom and Gomorrah look like a G-rated movie. I was bombarded with sexual propositions from key leaders, and harassment became a way of life. Thinking I might find some solidarity with the other women who worked there, I was heartbroken to find my overtures of friendship rudely rebuffed. I found out that many of these women had used less-than-virtuous methods to advance their careers, and they saw me as a threat to their territory.

I was overwhelmed professionally, terrified of going to work each day. I was playing with the "big boys," and I had no idea what the rules were. I felt as if I were always standing on shaky ground. Matthew 7:24–27 says a wise man builds his house on a rock. God is the Rock, the only place where we can stand firm and safe when the storms of life descend. Yet the foolish man builds on sand—his own strength, intellect and human wisdom. Not surprisingly, when the rain comes, his house is washed away.

I was foolish to take that job. If I had taken the time to place my new job before the Lord, I would have received

His guidance. I could have sought counsel from people who worked in similar situations, done more objective research on the city and the programs there, or even simply visited the office first before I accepted the position. I did not spy out the land, though, so I was completely unprepared for the giants that awaited me. No wonder I was standing on shifting sand, not solid rock. Worse yet, I allowed the battles on the job to distract me from my Kingdom purpose.

> A foolish man fails to seek and heed God's direction.

How do you receive the guidance you need to be better prepared for a new situation than I was? How do you know that the Lord wants you to move into a new job, transfer companies or even ask for a promotion? Usually, it is simple. God always gives direction to His people, and He always confirms His direction. If you follow basic biblical principles, you can be confident about receiving His direction. Here are a few things to help you build on rock, not sand:

1. Stay in a place of prayer about all of the things in your heart. This gives God time to speak to you about a new direction.
2. Stay in the Word of God. Sometimes God will highlight a passage of Scripture to you that you may have read several times before, but this time you know it directly applies to your new situation.
3. Seek counsel from godly people of good reputation. They can offer wisdom beyond your personal experience.
4. Listen and wait for the peace of God to confirm a decision. You may still feel a little nervous or uncertain, but God is faithful to quiet your heart.

I know that taking any of these steps would have protected me from my horrible experience. God is not trying to keep His will hidden from us. He is ready to guide us if we will only listen.

Conquering Fear

Missionaries must often trust God for their day-to-day survival. As a missionary in the marketplace, you must trust that when God sends you out, He will sustain you just as He sustained Caleb and Joshua, the two spies who came back to Moses with a good report. God knew the Israelites needed a homeland, so He prepared one for them. Likewise, God has prepared a special marketplace assignment just for you. As you learn to trust this reality, you will be better able to respond to the giants you are called to face.

You never know what is waiting for you at a new job. Sometimes the giant is a taste of the "real world," for which you are not quite ready. As a college student, I took a summer job in an office that was really one huge room divided into dozens of cubicles. Although we had our own work areas, I could hear everything going on with my new co-workers. At first I had to adjust to concentrating in the midst of the chatter and phone noise, but I settled in after a few days.

One afternoon I saw Mark from the accounting department approach our boss, Stewart, to discuss some financial statements. (Note that names and details have been changed throughout this book to protect those whose stories appear here.) A disagreement ensued, and the two men began arguing loudly. Everyone in the cubicles could hear everything they said, and it soon became clear that Stewart was out of control. His voice rose louder and angrier with each exchange. Then to everyone's shock, he grabbed Mark by the collar. Naturally we all got up from our cubicles to get a closer look at the heated exchange. Mark resisted Stewart's hold, but Stewart overpowered him and seemed ready to launch Mark out of a nearby window. Mercifully, two male co-workers tackled Stewart and freed Mark from his hands. They were actually forced to restrain Stewart until the police arrived.

Faith and fear are incompatible.

Stewart never returned to work; he had been drinking the day of the fight and had apparently been hiding a serious alcohol problem for many years. Not what I expected from the boss at my first professional office job! This experience, along with many others, helped me learn the importance of spying out the land. I had a lot to learn about the marketplace culture, let alone about how to share the Gospel without fear in such an environment.

Remember that all but two of the Israelite spies were paralyzed by fear. Fear in the marketplace can keep you from connecting with the right people, taking advantage of the right opportunities and ultimately fulfilling your purpose. This can happen in many ways:

1. *Bondage to the past.* In Philippians 3:13–14, Paul reminds us to leave the past behind us and focus on the finish line— the prize in Christ Jesus. *"Forgetting what is behind . . . I press on toward the goal,"* he said. Once you have repented of your sins, let them go. Do not let your past mistakes haunt you. God's mercies are new each morning!

2. *Believing the wrong report.* Sometimes the report of fear and faithlessness comes from those around us. People can speak thoughtless or cruel words to you or about you, but you do not need to receive them into your spirit. Remember to perform your marketplace assignment according to what *God* has said about you, not what people say.

3. *Failure to forgive.* As I mentioned briefly in chapter 1, many people who fail to forgive allow one or two bad experiences to ruin their attitude toward their job. Often they will bring baggage from an old job to a new one. On the other hand, if you forgive, you open the door for God to defend you. No matter what has been done to you, God's Word says He will repay you and restore that which has been stolen.

4. *Complacency.* Almost all of us have struggled with fear of the unknown at one time or another. This causes some Kingdom ambassadors in the marketplace to get stuck where they are comfortable instead of moving into the fresh calling God has for them, whether it is a professional advancement or a ministry opportunity. He desires that we remain yielded to the Spirit of God and move when He moves.

> Being stuck may be indicative of a failure to follow God's directions.

Receiving Your Marching Orders

I will never forget the first time my paycheck bounced. I was working for a well-known company in a fairly prominent position, yet none of us knew about the organization's financial problems until our paychecks started to come late and then finally started to bounce. I prayed fervently about this situation. I loved my job and felt a tremendous sense of purpose there, yet I knew in my spirit that if my employer was not satisfying his obligations to pay me, I had to leave. My husband and I had recently married, and we were struggling with household expenses and the costs related to my return to graduate school for a second degree.

In desperation, I cried out in prayer for confirmation: *God, if You want me to leave, please tell me clearly! Provide me with a job that will have an equally important mission, one that will enable me to help the people that I have been trained and prepared to help. And God, please make the transition to the new job an easy one.*

Within two days of that prayer, a job offer came from a very reputable company. I had interviewed with them some time ago, but had not heard anything. I returned to prayer, asking God to confirm that this position was the position He wanted me to take. Almost immediately, 2 Chronicles 20:17 came to my heart. I searched for it in my Bible:

> *You will not have to fight this battle. Take up your positions; stand firm and see the deliverance the Lord will give you, O Judah and Jerusalem. Do not be afraid; do not be discouraged. Go out to face them tomorrow, and the Lord will be with you.*

When I read that Scripture, I knew exactly what I was to do—*"take that position."* God often uses Scripture to give us direct words about situations we bring to Him in prayer. This verse was all the confirmation I needed. The next day I met with the president of the company where I was working to thank him for the opportunity to work with him and give him my two weeks' notice. I described the difficulty the paycheck situation had caused for me and other employees; I also offered to help him come up with a plan for resolving the company's financial challenges. He declined my offer.

Years later, I learned that the company had faced several lawsuits and eventually downsized nearly out of existence. It currently exists as a two-person office with a shady public reputation. The president is still there.

The Call to Be Righteously Strategic

To develop a righteously strategic approach to your marketplace assignment, you must understand what is expected of you on your job. Being righteously strategic means to discover prayerfully and respond to the requirements and expectations for your job and work environment in a thoughtful and prudent manner that is intentionally consistent with the Word of God.

Can you imagine a football player running onto the field without knowing what position he is supposed to play? Your role at work most likely involves expectations that are not articulated in your official job description. Does your new boss expect your reports to appear on her desk, or does she expect you to call and let her know they are there? Does your new boss make his deals in staff meetings or on the golf course? You cannot be so out of it that you do not understand the basics of how your workplace runs. You also cannot be so out of it that you do not know what God has called you to do there.

God has called us as His ambassadors in the marketplace to work among believers and unbelievers in a prudent and astute manner, without compromising our faith. That is one reason I quoted Matthew 10:16 earlier, which tells us to be as shrewd as snakes and as innocent as doves. Of course, God does not need our education or professional competence to accomplish the work of His Kingdom. Yet He gave us gifts and capabilities, and He provides opportunities to further develop these gifts and capabilities so that we can bring glory to Him in every area of our lives. Thinking and behaving in a righteously strategic manner helps us do our jobs better and avoid potentially dangerous situations.

I am glad that a few years into my career, I learned an important lesson about how being righteously strategic could help me avoid dangerous situations. An elected public official targeted me for his romantic advances, so he had me assigned to planning meetings and task force meetings that he chaired. As I prayed about my job each day, I began to sense that there was something less than innocent on his side during our interactions. I asked God to give me wisdom to know how to respond.

My sense of the Lord's leading was soon confirmed. A man I had never met approached me as I entered a building for a special meeting. He spoke to me as if we knew each other and quickly told me that the official's motives toward me were dishonorable. I was a little shaken by the exchange with this stranger, but what he told me confirmed what I was hearing from the Lord.

Once we learn, we must be ready to teach.

Strategically, I found reasons to avoid the official's meetings without making a scene. Eventually he got the message, and I no longer received invitations. Years later, that same official was exposed by the media in a major scandal. By seeking the Lord about my work, listening to His guidance and responding strategically, I was nowhere near the man at the time. I had left that dangerous situation far behind me.

Six Ways to Make Effective Job/Career Choices

It is important to be righteously strategic when searching for a new job or career. Here are some suggestions on remaining vigilant when it's your choice to explore new options or when faced with the loss of employment:

1. Reflect upon past difficulties and challenges God has delivered you from; then with a thankful heart, pray trusting God for the new job.
2. Renew your mind by reading the Bible and meditating upon Scriptures about God's faithfulness and provisions for His children.
3. Record the plan God gives you for your career search by writing it in a journal and revisiting it daily to document your actions taken.
4. Reinvent yourself. Acquire new skills through training and strengthen seldom used skills through temporary work and volunteer service.
5. Receive the help God provides. God may use people to give you wise counsel or to help you secure the job He has in store for you.
6. Rest as you wait with the knowledge that God is repositioning you for His next big assignment.

Guiding Fellow Believers

Sometimes you will need to offer insight to fellow believers who are "spying out the land" for themselves. Here are a few suggestions when offering guidance:

1. Offer only bite-sized and relevant information. Listen to the Holy Spirit for cues on what and how much to share. Trust that if the Lord intends to use you further in that individual's life, He will give you another opportunity to share.
2. Affirm the individual as you counsel or coach him or her. Always acknowledge strengths and growth, and let love motivate all your comments. When offering constructive

criticism, be sure to include suggestions with attainable strategies for growth. Use words that edify and instruct.
3. Pray for the individual. Spend time privately praying, but also, as the Holy Spirit leads you, pray with the person about whatever God reveals to you. If an idea the person shares with you seems unrealistic, pray that God will reveal it to him or her. Be careful not to destroy the "dream" that God may have planted in his or her heart.
4. Remain watchful and warn the individual when you see him or her approaching trouble. We will discuss the "watchman" role more in chapter 3.
5. Be transparent. Share your mistakes so others can benefit from the lessons you have learned. Resist the temptation to let someone else learn the hard way if you can share an experience that may help. Emphasize how God protected you when you were immature or ignorant, and share examples of His deliverance and victory in your life.
6. Project faith and not fear to an individual in need of your coaching. Remember, no matter how terrifying the giants in the land look, God has the power to liberate and deliver those who trust Him and apply His Word.

Laboring with the End in Mind

Ephesians 1:11 reminds us that God "works out everything in conformity with the purpose of his will." Understanding this helps us cooperate with God's plan and adjust our lives accordingly. God expects us to take what He has already given us in His Word as complete and adequate instruction on how to follow His plan. He wants to use us in the marketplace to proclaim the Gospel and to prepare the world for the return of Jesus.

Therefore, God is ordering our circumstances so that we might fulfill His purpose.

You are on a journey in this life, with God guiding your way. You need not worry—God has established your end. God is far more invested in your success than you are, so committing yourself completely to Him will only prosper you in the long run (see Deuteronomy 28:1–14). God wants you to prosper in all your ways. To do that, you must trust Him and believe He will lead you every step of the way.

When Joshua took over his new position as successor to Moses, he knew leading the Israelites would be no small task. It would be monumental—the biggest challenge of his life! How could anyone step into Moses' shoes (sandals) and not feel overwhelmed? Yet over and over God told Joshua, *"Be strong and courageous. . . . Be strong and very courageous."* God also told him, *"Do not be terrified; do not be discouraged, for the Lord your God will be with you wherever you go"* (Joshua 1:6–7, 9).

As with Joshua, God does not want you to be afraid. He has already set the time for your next promotion or new job and provided all the resources you need for success. Stay in prayer and in His Word, heed His voice, listen for His confirmation and prepare to go wherever He is sending you. As you do this, you will find that He is often calling you to places of leadership, as He did Joshua. We will look at the specifics of this marketplace calling in the next chapter.

Equipping Prayer

Heavenly Father, I am grateful for training that will allow me to become more spiritually aware at work. From this day forward, as I use the intellect and wisdom that You have given me, please let me not forsake the importance of being led by Your Holy Spirit. In the matchless name of Jesus I pray, Amen.

Marketplace Memory Scripture

Be strong and take heart, all you who hope in the Lord.

Psalm 31:24

Marketplace Experience Self-Evaluation

Record a time when you listened to someone's negative report about your job instead of listening to God.

Based on the teaching in chapter 2, list one biblical principle you could have applied to your work situation.

Why do you believe some Christians perceive work as a source of money and not as a form of ministry?

How do you demonstrate your love and fairness to believers and unbelievers in the marketplace?

Based on the teaching in chapter 2, rate your new skill level at taking Jesus to work and living out your faith on the job:

____ 1.   A Little Better Prepared
____ 2.   Much Better Prepared
____ 3.   Equipped

Note: *To increase your skill level after your initial reading of the chapter, please pray for wisdom according to James 1:5 and read the chapter again.*

3

Take Your Spot

"What are you waiting for, Ken?" I asked, mildly exasperated. This brilliant young man had just turned down his third offer of a prominent leadership position within our company. What made the situation more ridiculous was that we had been praying for months that God would provide a leadership opportunity for him.

"The positions seemed too good for me," he replied, looking down at his shoes as he spoke. "I really think God wants to give me an entry-level supervisory position . . . all these jobs are for middle managers. That would be too big a jump for me, don't you think?" he asked.

Three times God answered Ken's prayers that a position of leadership would open, but each time, Ken felt unprepared to proceed. His preconceived ideas about how God should bless him prevented him from taking possession of the territory God was offering him.

As God's ambassador in the marketplace, you must be prepared to boldly go wherever God is calling you, even if the place is unfamiliar or unexpected. Ken was so focused on his natural abilities that he could not see the supernatural power of God at work in his life. He knew God had sent him those offers, but he lacked the courage to accept them. I believe many Christians are in need of more courage to accept the leadership roles, formal or spiritual, that God is offering them in the marketplace.

By no means do I discount the reality that any kind of leadership responsibility is a challenge. It is always easier remaining in the background, doing the basics and collecting your paycheck. I also realize that some less mature believers will jump at certain opportunities prematurely and make a mess of them. The real issue I am addressing here, however, is that we need to recognize that God has called us as Christians to lead wherever we are, including at work. Sometimes we will lead in a spiritual position simply by serving others. Sometimes we will lead in a more formal position by setting the agenda, controlling the budget and planning the strategy for the next five years. Whatever our specific position in the marketplace, God is calling us to lead with righteousness and integrity.

Jesus was the ultimate leader, and His life is our model of righteousness. He taught and modeled righteousness for both the multitudes and for His disciples, but the disciples' contact with Him was up close and personal—every day, they saw how His public and private character were one and the same. To them, He

PRAYER POINT: Pray for knowledge to discern how you can effectively apply biblical principles to every situation you face.

Heavenly Father, please grant me the daily knowledge that I am on display for the good of the Kingdom of God. In all earnestness, help me model Christ's example of being a servant, friend and leader. In Jesus' name I pray, Amen.

> God has called us as Christians to lead wherever we are, including at work.

explained and demonstrated how to live a life wholly given over to God, a life that in every respect accurately represented God's character.

Jesus expects no less of Christians today. He wants us to be righteous representatives of His authority through both our words and actions. Our professional lives should exemplify the nature and character of God and draw attention to His Kingdom, and our personal lives should do no less. God calls us to influence everyone around us toward coming to a saving knowledge of Jesus Christ.

Open to God's Will

In the last chapter, we learned the importance of spying out the land and preparing for whatever lies ahead. We need to be careful, however, not to become bound to a particular course of action while we are in the preparation stage. Have you ever researched a major purchase like a computer so carefully that you went to the store knowing the precise model number you wanted? Now suppose that when you visited the store, the manager explained that a newer model with more features was on sale for the same price you were prepared to pay. At first glance, the change in plans may have seemed more trouble than it was worth. You had

> A narrow view of God's ability to use us will limit our leaps of faith.

not researched this newer product. Would it meet all your needs? Was this salesman just trying to unload the last ten units of another model to make his quota?

These are all legitimate questions to ask yourself in such a scenario. If you are unwilling to tackle them, though, you might miss out on a terrific bargain. My friend Ken was so fixated on an introductory position that he could not bring himself to accept a middle management job, even the third time it was offered! Middle management was not what Ken felt prepared for, but in his case it was a terrific bargain—the favor of God. He forgot that he was fearfully and wonderfully made, the work of God's hands, God's heir and part of God's eternal purpose (see Psalm 139:14; 2 Corinthians 3:18; Galatians 4:7; Ephesians 2:10). His narrow view of God's ability to use him limited him to taking small steps. He was unprepared for the large leap of faith God had in store for him.

God's Word declares His response to the obedient and the disobedient.

So many Christians live below their potential, just as Ken did, because they do not believe they deserve a promotion or a new job. Maybe they do not think they have earned it because of their past mistakes. Remember who our God is, though—He is a loving Father who wants to give gifts to His children. Each of His gifts has a purpose. To walk as a faithful Kingdom worker in the marketplace, you must accept the position that God has for you as His gift to you. Do not allow your past, fear or even pride to convince you otherwise.

Uprooting the Blind Leader

God's Word reminds us that His redemptive plan for humanity includes removing the unrighteous from leadership and placing those who obey Him in authority. Consider what Jesus said in Matthew 15:13–14: *"Every plant that my heavenly Father has not planted will be pulled up by the roots. Leave them; they are blind guides. If a blind man leads a blind man, both will fall into a pit."*

The world is full of blind leaders who are leading unsuspecting followers into ditches. In this parable, Jesus exhorts us not to worry about it. Anything God has not planted will eventually be uprooted by God Himself. This is true everywhere, including in our professional environments. Our duty is to be ready to take our place of leadership when that uprooting occurs.

God hates wickedness and unrighteousness everywhere, including in the business world. The Bible reminds us that *"when the righteous are in authority, the people rejoice"* (Proverbs 29:2, KJV). For the sake of both His people and unbelievers, God is unseating many of the wicked who have held positions of authority. These "shake-ups" open opportunities to God's people who are prepared to step up to the challenge. God will grant leadership to those He trusts, even when, like Ken, they may not possess all the qualifications in the natural realm.

Thousands of objections may echo in your head when you consider the call to lead in the marketplace: *But I'm just out of college. But I'm only the secretary. But I'm twenty years younger (or twenty years older) than everyone else.* All these objections can be summed up in the question, *Why should anyone listen to me?*

The call to fulfill God's Kingdom purposes will always seem staggering in comparison to your natural abilities to perform it.

The first answer for that is, Why not? God has shown us time and time again that He elevates whomever He wishes for His own pleasure and glory. God raised up Gideon in a time when His people needed inspiration. Gideon perceived himself as an average man of no particular distinction, and he seriously questioned the call: *"But Lord,"* Gideon asked, *"how can I save Israel? My clan is the weakest in Manasseh, and I am the least in my family"* (see Judges 6:15). Yet God saw so much more ability in Gideon than Gideon could see in himself. God used a man who had little confidence in his own abilities to perform a great and mighty work.

God uses equally "average" Christians today in the same way and qualifies them for the special work at hand. As there was a call on Gideon's life, there is a call on your life, too. And keep in mind that the call always relates more to God's Kingdom purposes than to your personal qualifications or lack thereof!

We are often tempted to restrict our efforts to reach and influence nonbelievers to the context of formal ministry activities: church, Bible study and so on. Yet those activities represent just a tiny fraction of our lives each week. Most of us spend the vast majority of our waking hours at work. Should we not focus at least some of our evangelistic efforts on this time as well?

We need to remember that the marketplace is far more than just the center of our economic activity. People take home to their families and communities the thoughts and viewpoints they are exposed to at work. Jesus understood this, which is why we see so many biblical accounts of Him ministering in the marketplace. It is the place not only where people work, but where people search for answers. Jesus understood that the health of the marketplace corresponded to the health of a society. And if a righteous standard is to be raised where people work, there must be righteous people there to raise it and lead others.

In my earliest faith-sharing experiences in the marketplace, I was often ostracized because I was extremely candid and vocal about my faith and intolerant of unrighteous conduct and practices. My job was never in jeopardy, but my superiors excluded me from projects and planning sessions that were not part of my regular duties, and my co-workers failed to invite me to special celebrations that were work related. Although my diligence and competence were unquestioned by superiors and co-workers, they made certain that I understood I was not a "member of the club."

After a few such occurrences, I began to realize that my effectiveness for God in the marketplace was being thwarted because I had not learned how to become righteously strategic (see again Matthew 10:16). Through prayer and meditation, God gave me righteous strategies for the marketplace. They are scattered throughout this book, but here are some of primary importance in a difficult work environment:

1. Try to restrict most discussions about faith to breaks and lunchtimes, which are traditionally perceived as personal time by most companies. Take a look at chapter 6 and my experience with Susan.
2. Identify the loner in your workplace and invite him or her to share a brown-bag lunch. Your show of interest might open up an opportunity for a discussion about your faith.
3. Ask God for the discernment to know which co-workers need extra prayer on a particular day. A timely comment of interest in them and their workload might have an amazing impact on their willingness to let you inside the walls of their heart.
4. When you make mistakes, publicly apologize to those in your work group and offer a corrective action plan. When others see your frailties and your willingness to take responsibility for your actions, they will be amazed at your character and integrity.
5. Go the extra mile in performing your work, be excited about your work and maintain a heart of gratitude about it, whether the assignment is large or small, difficult or easy. Co-workers will admire your steadfastness and diligence, which may lead to opportunities for you to share your faith with them.

6. Find direct and indirect ways of acknowledging God's presence in your life. Always give God credit for the successes you experience.

7. Ask God to help you establish a high standard of excellence pleasing to Him, and then maintain it (see Colossians 3:23). God gave Daniel, Hananiah, Mishael and Azariah a standard of excellence that enabled them to be "ten times better" in wisdom and understanding than anyone else in the king's service (see Daniel 1:17–20). If you are willing and obedient, God will give you knowledge and understanding that may make you appear to others in your workplace as "ten times better," too, which is an attractive trait that will draw others to Christ.

8. Find out who is watching you and mentor them. Through contact with you, they will be changed.

9. Ask God for the grace to help target those you are to influence. Look for those who seem receptive to you and begin there (see chapter 1, prayer point 5).

10. Learn to look at people as if they are being transformed and always acknowledge the progress they are making.

11. Help someone with his or her work without being asked, and do not tell anyone else that you did.

12. Ask God to instruct you about how to express biblical truths without depending on "religious" language (see chapter 1, prayer point 2). I use business vernacular when referring to the wisdom in a biblical story or Scripture.

13. Make certain your speech reflects your Christian conduct and character. A female unbeliever in the ladies' restroom at work turned to me and made a sarcastic remark about a woman who had just left the restroom: "Every other word out of her mouth is 'Praise the Lord!'" I smiled and excitedly exclaimed, "Yes, that's right! Praise the Lord! I believe in praising the Lord, too." Immediately she replied,

"But at least you act like a Christian instead of just saying the words."

14. "Make the most of every opportunity" to express your faith, letting your conversation and other contacts with unbelievers *"be always full of grace, seasoned with salt"* (Colossians 4:6). I always accompany my gifts to people at the office with a card that not only expresses my good wishes but also mentions my faith, sometimes directly and sometimes indirectly.

15. Express interest in the personal lives of your co-workers if they are open to sharing with you. I visit co-workers and/or their significant loved ones when they are in the hospital, and before leaving, I ask if I can pray for them. I attend the funerals of my co-workers' significant loved ones, which often results in opportunities to talk with them about Christ.

16. Invite your co-workers to attend Christian special events, especially those events involving you or your family. They are often willing to come and are honored that you would invite them. I extend invitations for co-workers to come hear me or my husband speak, or hear a special speaker. I use the term *speak* instead of *preach* when I invite them, and then I give them the time and location. I have also invited folks to come see my daughter dance or see my son in a play.

> Righteous people must raise a righteous standard at work, too.

17. Times may come when God requires us to stand, speak and act as His representatives in the workplace even if it jeopardizes our employment, relationships or popularity. (I relate some of my own such experiences in chapters 7 and 8.) Our obedience to God in such times must be unwavering.

Respecting Authority

To excel as effective leaders in the marketplace, believers must also show themselves as faithful followers. They must know how to respond appropriately to those in authority over them, whatever situation arises. It is so easy to forget that our bosses are human, too. They can seem either aloof and removed from our day-to-day lives, or wealthy and invulnerable. Yet our bosses need God just like everyone else does. Christians in the workplace should be known for both respecting and having compassion for those in leadership over them.

As a member of the senior management team for a large association, I learned this in dramatic fashion. Our CEO was a gregarious man, a typical power player without a care in the world. He was tall and broad-shouldered, and the graying at his temples detracted nothing from his smile and commanding personality. One day we gathered for our monthly team meeting. We took our places around the conference table, exchanging pleasantries until the CEO arrived. Although he was normally at least fifteen minutes early, this particular day he arrived just before the meeting began. He launched into his customary overview of what the meeting would cover, then he stopped mid-sentence. He stared out the window fixedly, his mouth slightly open.

No one said anything, and the silence continued. Each of us felt more uncomfortable by the minute. The pause was finally broken when the CEO began to cry. His whimper quickly became an uncontrolled sobbing. Naturally, we were all taken aback. To my dismay, many of the startled faces around the table quickly turned to expressions of disgust, as though they were appalled at his outburst. My heart ached for my boss, and I began praying under my breath for him to be shielded from further embarrassment. Moved by the Spirit of God, I stood to my feet and began to applaud him. I do not know how long it was until others joined me, but eventually we were all standing. The CEO composed himself, thanked us for the support and ended the meeting. (Later, we found out that the reason behind his outburst was an unwelcome change of positions in the works, which meant we would be losing him as our CEO.)

This was a moment when I had to lead by example. It would have been entirely inappropriate for me to explain to everyone what I thought a proper response was to our boss's emotional display. Yet by responding to the Lord, I was able to *show* others how we could behave righteously and respectfully, and they followed my lead. My actions defused the tense situation and allowed our leader to save face in the midst of his crisis.

Understanding Influence

Jesus modeled for us all the characteristics of walking out a faith-filled life as a missionary in the marketplace. First, He worked diligently under authority as a carpenter in Joseph's business. Later, He traveled through many different environments and called His twelve disciples out of their various professions. He also used numerous examples from the marketplace in his teachings and parables—for example, the farmer sowing seeds, the laborers in the vineyard, the wise and foolish investing of the talents and the shrewd estate manager (see Matthew 13:1–9; 20:1–16; 25:14–30; Luke 16:1–9). It seems fair to say that Jesus spent as much of His earthly ministry in the marketplace as He did teaching in the synagogues. He had broad influence and appeal in the marketplace and used it skillfully to further His Father's Kingdom.

Leaders are by definition a rare breed. Most people are followers. Leaders do not even need a formal position of authority to exert influence on those around them. If a few popular kids in high school start wearing a certain kind of jeans or shoes, hundreds of others will eventually follow. God teaches Christians to neither shun nor be enamored with leaders—He reminds us that He Himself is not a respecter of persons (see Acts 10:34). Yet as we fearlessly speak the truth to leader and follower alike, we find that God arranges an audience for us with people of influence so that we can follow Jesus' example and influence them for God's Kingdom.

Paul understood this when he survived a shipwreck on his way to stand trial before the emperor of Rome. God allowed Paul to go through countless trials because He knew Paul was fearless enough to share the Gospel with the most powerful political ruler of his day: *"The following night, the Lord stood near Paul and said, 'Take courage! As you have testified about me in Jerusalem, so you must also testify in Rome'"* (Acts 23:11). Under the influence of Paul and other early believers, the Roman Empire would never be the same. Three centuries later, the Roman emperor himself would declare allegiance to Jesus Christ.

> To evangelize anywhere is to be a leader.

Likewise, the disciples touched the life of a wealthy businesswoman, Lydia, who the Bible says was "a dealer in purple cloth." When Lydia believed and was baptized, "the members of her household were baptized" along with her (Acts 16:14–15). Her entire household followed her example!

To evangelize anywhere is to be a leader. Using your God-given influence, you are asking people around you to follow you to your Savior. God has placed many people on your job specifically so they can receive His touch through you. Will you win them if you are only a follower?

The Mandate for Righteous Leadership

This must sound basic and simplistic, but Christians must lead—righteously. We see throughout the Bible that God was always honored when His people led others in paths of righteousness. When His people failed to fulfill their assignment, they were uprooted and relieved of their duty.

Samson is a prime example of a leader who was released from his assignment when he violated his covenant with God (see Judges 16). King Saul also began his reign with God's grace and favor, but God uprooted him after his rebellion and disobedience and replaced him with King David (see 1 Samuel 15). We should not think that God will set a different standard for each of us. God is still replacing unrepentant and disobedient leaders today.

Obedience to God's will and active engagement in the assignment He has given you is the key to being deemed trustworthy by God to lead. The wonderful news is that when you cooperate with God's plan, you cannot help but reap favor and success. The blessings God desires to shower on you will cause members of your community, your church, your family and even your co-workers to be dumbfounded by the amazing way God uses you in your faithfulness.

> Uncompromising marketplace service pleases God.

The more Christians embrace their ministry responsibility in the marketplace and live out their faith in an uncompromising manner, the more incredible success they will realize individually, collectively and for the Kingdom of God. Consider the Christian music industry. It was a tiny industry only a couple of decades ago. According to the Gospel Music Association, sales of Christian music increased 80 percent during the first ten years that the industry was tracked (1995–2005). The Christian movie industry displays a similar success story. Today, Christian movies with tiny budgets have begun to astound investors with their profitability.

I believe that such Christian industries and businesses will continue to prosper. And most importantly, more and more unbelievers will accept Jesus as their Savior as a result. Whatever industry you work in, God wants you to aspire to heights of greatness as a living epistle in the marketplace. He will make that possible as long as you are righteous, faithful and obedient.

You cannot lead people if you are governed by the same things that govern them, though. You cannot lead others in the marketplace if you are driven by money, worldly success and fame. You must possess a love for God that transcends your need for these things, your love for yourself and even your love for others. God cannot greatly use you if you are preoccupied with your wants and your needs. Although the secondary benefits of work allow you to enjoy the fruits of your labor—supporting yourself and your family—and to sow your time, talents and money into your local church, your first responsibility in the marketplace is to work obediently to please God.

One of the ways we obediently work to please God is by following His instructions. Remember the imagery Jesus used in the parable of the ten pounds to explain how we were to wait until His return? He told us, *"Occupy till I come"* (Luke 19:13, KJV). That word *occupy* is used in a military sense, meaning "to maintain control over a certain territory, to keep things in order." To occupy anywhere, including in the marketplace, we need to make sure we have the correct orders from our commander. We cannot occupy territory God has not delegated to us.

This means you and I must be willing to give up anything, including professional prestige or a great-paying job, on a moment's notice if God says so. If He has sent us somewhere, we will possess the grace to occupy in that place. When the grace lifts, you and I must move with God, just as the Israelites moved with the cloud they followed by day as they wandered in the wilderness: *"By day the Lord went ahead of them in a pillar of cloud to guide them on their way and by night in a pillar of fire to give them light, so that they could travel by day or night"* (Exodus 13:21).

> When we are committed to working for God in the marketplace, we occupy and move as He leads.

God is still leading His people today. There is nothing accidental or coincidental about His leadership. I have marveled for years at the positions of authority in which God has placed me. Over the years, I began to understand that my assignment was similar to that of many of God's leaders in the Bible. I was often called to transition into a position quickly, bring order to chaos, declare salvation to the lost and through my work style bring conviction to the wicked. And I am no different than you—as I said earlier, God is no respecter of persons. If God could use me, given my failings and inadequacies, He can use any willing and submitted vessel. As He did with His leaders of old, He may also call you to bring order, declare salvation and bring conviction wherever He places you.

I would have been more comfortable in the background, as you may be, learning the ropes and praying in secret. If I had chosen my role or written the script, it would have progressed much differently than how it actually worked out. God Almighty, however, was the writer and director. He has a plan, a purpose and a destiny, and it is up to me to submit accordingly.

It is also up to you. When you see your role at work as occupying territory for the Savior instead of as a stepping-stone in your personal agenda, you learn to let go. I had to let go of my personal ambitions, and I found them gradually replaced with God's ambitions. The wonderful part is that I ended up advancing more quickly in my career as I followed God's leading than

I would have if I had chosen the path on my own. Not only did my career "take off," but so did my faith in what God could do through me. I learned that letting go means that everything must be all about God. *"What good will it be for a man if he gains the whole world, yet forfeits his soul?"* Matthew 16:26 asks, *"Or what can a man give in exchange for his soul?"*

The enemy will always try to seduce us with fame, prestige, money and power. Remember that the devil's goal is to destroy the plans of God and destroy those who belong to God. Almost all of us have been in a place of financial need at one time or another, so it is vital that we abide in the richness of God, who owns the earth and the cattle on a thousand hills (see Psalm 24:1; 50:10). When we recognize that every bit of our professional success comes from God, we give Him glory for all the witty strategies and inventions that come to us (see Proverbs 8:12), and for all the inspiration and status. When we prove ourselves trustworthy with a measure of authority, God will release us to greater and greater works (see Luke 19:17).

The Marketplace Watchman

Levels of spiritual leadership exist in the marketplace, just as they do in the local church. When you have shown yourself a faithful example of the qualities mentioned in the previous section, you will likely find that God is ready to entrust even more authority to you. You may receive a promotion in the natural realm, moving to a managerial or even an executive position. However, you may also find yourself promoted spiritually to a role I like to call the "marketplace watchman."

The purpose of the marketplace watchman is to protect and comfort others by being alert to danger or drastic transition that may loom on the horizon. Remember that the average people in your workplace view their jobs as their source of income and sustenance. Therefore, any instability in your company or organization has the potential to strike terror into their hearts. When you function in the role of the marketplace watchman, in addition to exemplifying Jesus' character, you also begin to serve as a prophetic voice in the midst of potential storms.

The marketplace watchman is a spiritual leader who protects, comforts and warns others.

I remember spending a week in intensive prayer one time after God gave me Psalm 127:1 in my spirit: *"Except the Lord build the house, they labour in vain that build it: except the Lord keep the city, the watchman waketh but in vain"* (KJV). I knew this Scripture related somehow to the organization in which I had been a key leader for a number of years. My intensive time of prayer eventually went on for several more weeks as I realized that God wanted to reveal some crushing news to me about this organization.

During this time, I kept receiving Psalm 127:1 as I prayed. Out of my concern, I beseeched God for mercy, even as I sensed in my spirit that God was going to judge the principal leader and the entire organization for blatant and unrepentant acts of unrighteousness. I asked God what He would have me do. He led me to pray aggressively that He would prepare my colleagues for the events that were imminent. I took advantage of every opportunity that I had to share Christ with my colleagues and to help them to understand the importance of trusting God in good times and bad.

Within five months, the principal leader of our organization was publicly exposed and made to give an account for his shameful behavior. Not only did he lose his position, but the entire organization was shut down. My colleagues who had accepted Christ were more readily able to transition to other pursuits and move on with their lives. Everyone else who was spiritually unprepared experienced an extremely difficult time regrouping, although they eventually managed. Perhaps more importantly, those of us who trusted God through the ordeal rejoiced in our deliverance and provision from the hand of God. Everyone else seemed to become bitter and resentful.

Just as the ancient watchmen of Israel were positioned high above the city to see beyond the average man's range of vision, so you will be set above the downsizing, firings, managerial changes and executive shake-ups unless God allows them in your life for your good and His glory (see Romans 8:28 and my personal experience with downsizing in chapter 10). You will be a source of stability and peace to those around you, and you will be able to offer counsel and guidance. You do not have to worry whether or not people listen to you. God says your role is only to speak the truth.

Son of man, I have made you a watchman for the house of Israel; so hear the word I speak and give them warning from me. When I say to the wicked, "O wicked man, you will surely die," and you do not speak out to dissuade him from his ways, that wicked man will die for his sin, and I will hold you accountable for his blood. But if you do warn the wicked man to turn from his ways and he does not do so, he will die for his sin, but you will have saved yourself.

Ezekiel 33:7–9

One of the most critical aspects of the watchman's responsibilities is to warn unbelieving individuals about their unrighteous lifestyles and to warn the general population of imminent danger. I believe many Christians called as watchmen in the marketplace are failing in their assignments, often for one of two reasons. The first reason is fear. They may fear for their jobs, their popularity or their respect from people, or they may fear that they will say the wrong things. The second reason I have observed that

> The marketplace watchman must issue God's warnings without thought of self-protection.

potential watchmen fail the Lord is indifference. They truly do not care if the people God has appointed them to watch over suffer or die in their sins.

Leadership is a privilege that comes with God-given requirements. God expects us to hear His voice, read His Word and communicate His truth without fear. When God alerts us to danger on the horizon, He expects us to issue His warnings. These warnings may relate to the integrity of the operations in a particular workplace, the impact that the mission and vision of a company or organization may have on society or on a people group, a word about a pending conflict or a cautionary word to the people about an individual or collective sin pattern. Whatever the specific situation, we watchmen must sound the alarm lest the blood of those around us end up on our hands! I have learned not to worry too much about whether my warnings are heeded, as long as I obey God by giving them.

Wanda cleaned our offices at night so she could take college courses during the day. She and I prayed together often. One night, she told me she was worried because she suspected that her boss was stealing from some of the businesses where they had cleaning contracts. She had no tangible proof, so we prayed about it.

Eventually, Wanda obtained direct evidence of her boss's stealing. I warned her to speedily report the situation to her boss's superior and to request reassignment to another supervisor. Unfortunately, she was afraid of losing her job. We continued to pray about the situation, and because I sensed in my spirit that she was running out of time to make her decision, I continued to exhort Wanda to take action.

Wanda never did take action, but the stealing did become public. An official investigation was launched into certain missing items that eventually were connected to her company. Since she was one of three other people who had access to the offices where the items were reported missing, her boss shifted the blame for the thefts to her. Wanda was placed on leave without pay pending the outcome of the police investigation.

My heart broke for her. I wished she had heeded my warnings, but I had done my part to deliver them. I continued to pray for God's mercy for her, however. After several weeks of inquiry, an investigation and missed pay, Wanda was able to prove her innocence by explaining what she had seen in her boss's possession. She was eventually exonerated, and she returned to her job under a new supervisor.

Remember that as God calls you to lead—especially as a marketplace watchman—He will give you special wisdom to do so. As you perform your work with excellence, remember to listen closely for His voice. In the next chapter, we will discover how to remain focused and faithful to His call.

———————————*Equipping Prayer*———————————

Heavenly Father, please forgive me for getting so caught up with the busyness of the moment that I fail to heed Your direction and Your warnings for myself and my co-workers. Please help me to work with the realization that You are my top priority and that I live to serve You. In the magnificent name of Jesus I pray, Amen.

——————— Marketplace Memory Scripture ———————

This is what the Lord Almighty says: "Administer true justice; show mercy and compassion to one another."
Zechariah 7:9

Marketplace Experience Self-Evaluation

Record a time when God gave you forewarning about a marketplace situation involving a boss, a co-worker, the company or just yourself.

Based on the teaching in chapter 3, list one biblical principle you could have applied to that situation.

What are some ways that people violate justice, mercy and compassion in your industry?

How can a Christian be both ethical and profitable?

Based on the teaching in chapter 3, rate your new skill level at taking Jesus to work and living out your faith on the job:

    ___ 1.   A Little Better Prepared
    ___ 2.   Much Better Prepared
    ___ 3.   Equipped

Note: *To increase your skill level after your initial reading of the chapter, please pray for wisdom according to James 1:5 and read the chapter again.*

4

Fix Your Focus

Have you ever been driving somewhere without having a clear idea of where you are going? You read the street signs, hoping that something will look familiar. You make U-turns and check the map, all the time using up gas and getting frustrated. It is so much easier when you have the exact address, the precise directions or even one of those GPS devices to tell you where to go.

As God's representative in the marketplace, you must also have a clear idea of where you are going. You need to have a firm grasp of the big picture expressed in Romans 8:28: *"And we know that all things work together for good to them that love God, to them who are the called according to his purpose"* (KJV). "His purpose" is your big-picture assignment—to bring God glory and expand His Kingdom.

You also need a strong sense of your responsibilities at work and how they fit into that big picture. The various tasks that comprise your assignments every day are passing and brief in comparison with what you accomplish for eternity. No matter how long its tenure, earthly work is always short-term compared to the work of God's Kingdom. Still, God has ordained you to

PRAYER POINT: Pray for knowledge to fulfill God's purpose in the marketplace.

Heavenly Father, please make me sensitive to the needs of the company and my co-workers. Teach me how to reflect Your presence so that I will see, understand and respond to my co-workers through eyes of love. Let me conduct myself in a manner that will cause them to be receptive to hearing about You. In Jesus' name I pray, Amen.

fulfill His larger purpose through your faithfulness in such smaller, earthly tasks. This conviction will propel you to complete an assignment even if it is inconvenient or difficult. It will set you apart from others who are only working for recognition or pay. At some point in life, everyone is faced with a task that does not seem worth the trouble. At those times, God's purpose will give you the extra motivation you need to do the job and do it well, keeping in mind your faithfulness in the little things goes beyond the temporal realm into the eternal.

Eyes to See

Understanding and operating in God's purpose requires two things: vision and hearing. Proverbs 29:18 reminds us, *"Where there is no vision, the people perish: but he that keepeth the law, happy is he"* (KJV). A small event in my life brought home to me the importance of vision. My eyes had been bothering me quite a bit. I had been reading a lot, and the time I spent staring at the computer screen was not doing my sight any favors, either. After a few weeks of headaches, I finally decided to get my eyes examined.

The ophthalmologist ran a series of tests, the last of which involved the dilation of my eyes. After an hour, the doctor had all the information he needed. He prescribed some reading glasses for me, which he felt would relieve my vision problems and headaches. His assistant then gave me some strange-looking sunglasses to wear and sent me on my way. The dilation had made my eyes extra sensitive to light, so the sunglasses were meant to protect them.

> Spiritual vision can become distorted when we lose our anchor in God's purpose.

Unwisely, I tried to drive myself home. *After all,* I thought, *the route is familiar to me, and there is not much traffic. I will be fine.* As I pulled out onto the road, I noticed immediately that my eyesight was extremely limited. I could only see things directly in front of me; if I tried to peer out much farther or use my peripheral vision, objects became distorted almost beyond recognition. Just the smallest amount of strain caused my head to ache as well. This was a little alarming, to say the least, but I managed to make it home safely.

Just as dilating my eyes distorted my natural vision, I believe losing our anchor in God's purpose can distort our spiritual vision. Praise God that He understands our limitations. That is why He instructs us to keep our eyes firmly fixed on Him: *"So we fix our eyes not on what is seen, but on what is unseen. For what is seen is temporary, but what is unseen is eternal"* (2 Corinthians 4:18). When we remain focused on God, we will see Him in the midst of our stormy days and our calm days. We will ignore things that attempt to obstruct our view of God and our role in helping fulfill His Kingdom work in the earth. We want 20/20 spiritual vision, so we must look to God and faithfully move forward in Him.

If you have ever taught a teenager to drive, you know that one of the most important lessons you can teach is *keep your eyes on the road!* While we may occasionally need to turn and check a blind spot, for the most part we need to face forward. This does not mean, however, that we should be oblivious to what is around us. The rearview and side view mirrors allow us to remain aware of our surroundings while staying focused on where we are going. Obviously, it would be dangerous to drive staring out the side window instead of the windshield. In the same way, we run great risk in life when we spend too much time looking backward, to the left or to the right.

To stay focused, we must block out distractions.

Part of staying focused on God means knowing which aspects of our surroundings to react to and which are mere distractions or hindrances. When we are behind the wheel, a car veering into our lane requires a reaction from us, while a roadside carnival does not. Yet I have found that too many marketplace missionaries get into costly accidents because they are paying too much attention to a distraction that has nothing to do with them. Is there an interoffice conflict that does not involve you? It is probably wisest to stay out of it. Are there rumors of layoffs in the next quarter? You may want to make sure your resume is updated, but other than that, you have no control over what will happen. You need to stay focused on the road God has you on now because it is not yet time to turn right or left. Staying focused means not just looking forward at God but also deliberately blocking out distractions that surround you.

Ears to Hear

The sheep listen to his voice. He calls his own sheep by name and leads

70

them out. When he has brought out all his own, he goes on ahead of them, and his sheep follow him because they know his voice. But they will never follow a stranger; in fact, they will run away from him because they do not recognize a stranger's voice.

John 10:3–5

Jesus used this parable of the sheep to illustrate how we follow Him in a hostile world full of false shepherds and "strangers." Sheep have excellent hearing, and marketplace missionaries must work to develop their hearing as well. We need to hear the voice of our Shepherd over the clamor of society's expectations, our unregenerate flesh and the countless "voices of strangers" that call to us every day. Sometimes a stranger's voice may not be overtly evil; it is simply a voice other than our Shepherd's.

I can recall times when I accepted a job or ministry assignment that was not within God's purpose for me. These positions involved work of tremendous value to the Kingdom of God, but they were not the specific assignments God had ordained for me. Although my intentions were noble, the tasks required greater (or different) grace than had been apportioned to me for that season in my life. Thus my efforts bore little fruit, and I became frustrated. Had I listened more closely to my Shepherd's voice, I would have been planted in a more fruitful vineyard—the place God had for me. Instead, I was occupying a place God had prepared for someone else.

> God will use every mistake as a "teachable moment."

Despite these momentary setbacks, God redeemed my time. I believe God honors our intentions, even when we neglect to listen closely. God will redeem your time, too, if you have made similar decisions. Ultimately, because of God's mercy, nothing is lost in His economy. God will use every mistake as a "teachable moment" and grant us a greater level of dependence on Him.

It takes time and effort to keep our eyes fixed on Jesus and our ears trained to hear His voice. Yet it is more than worth the effort. We must be resolute in our efforts to remain in constant fellowship with God so that we can follow His leading. As Oswald Chambers puts it in his book *My Utmost for His Highest*, "The call of God is like the call of the sea; no one hears it but the one who has the nature of the sea in him." The more the nature of God is in us, the more naturally we will hear His call.

We need to develop our hearing for more than just making major decisions for the future. As we focus on the Lord and listen to His voice, we also gain clarification about our current assignment. He can also give us midcourse corrections if our marching orders change or if we start to veer off course. God enables us to hear and respond as His purpose unfolds for us.

Accepting Your Assignment

Many years ago, a faithful Christian named Ruth served as a registered nurse in the operating room of the most active trauma hospital in the country at that time. She worked overtime frequently and often felt overwhelmed by the demanding nature of her job. Weary and facing burnout, Ruth traded her work at the trauma hospital for a more low-key nursing position at a specialized center. Not long after leaving her old position, she realized she had made a mistake. The job at the trauma hospital was the place God had planted her. Ruth prayed for divine understanding regarding her career, and God clarified His purpose for her in her original position.

With renewed passion, Ruth returned to the trauma hospital and excelled in her work. She also excelled in taking Jesus to work. She always made it a point to model the care and compassion that she would want to receive if she were in the patients' shoes. She ministered the saving grace of Jesus Christ to those near death's door, including the most horrendous cases of gunshot or stabbing wounds and drug overdoses. Ruth consoled families who were in deep despair and held the hands of many who were lonely or fearful. She also encouraged and prayed for her co-workers when they felt tired or weary. Ruth wound up becoming an outspoken and effective advocate for high-quality patient care. She was an amazing model of

> Following the Lord will require childlike obedience and submission to the Holy Spirit.

a marketplace missionary for me and for countless others. Ruth was also my mother.

As He sent my mother, God is sending you and me into our places of work so we can confront the powers of darkness with the Gospel of Christ. Your gender, your race, your gifts and your talents are all part of how God has formed you to have a special impact on people who need your unique qualities. It may be hard to understand sometimes, but God's thoughts and ways are always higher than our thoughts and ways (see Isaiah 55:8–9). God is simply waiting for you to take the position He has ordained for you. And if you know you are already in the position God has ordained for you, then He desires for you to approach your responsibilities in a righteously strategic manner and step into whatever leadership roles He opens for you. He wants you to take the step that sets you apart from others and live out your faith in your place of employment.

A. W. Tozer puts it this way in *The Pursuit of God*:

> As the sailor locates his position on the sea by "shooting" the sun, so we may get our moral bearings by looking at God. We must

begin with God. We are right when and only when we stand in a right position relative to God, and we are wrong so far and so long as we stand in any other position.

Once you begin this journey, you will find that your spiritual compass will align with that of the "Navigator of your soul," and you will be on course for God's purpose.

Walking with Focus

A focused walk with God has certain qualities, particularly in the marketplace. God has prepared good works for us in advance, and He expects us to walk worthily of the calling (see Ephesians 2:10; 4:1). We are to walk as children of light (see Ephesians 5:8). We are to walk carefully, not as the unwise, but as the wise (see Ephesians 5:15). We are to walk in a manner that will please God so that we may abound more and more (see 1 Thessalonians 4:1).

A focused walk will bear fruit. John 15:8 reminds us, *"This is to my Father's glory, that you bear much fruit, showing yourselves to be my disciples."* Through purposeful holy living, we lead others to Christ and become more like Him. Following the Lord deliberately requires childlike obedience and submission to the Holy Spirit. Consider for a moment how young children tend to interact with their parents. When a toddler wants out of the high chair, she simply reaches her arms toward Mom. Then Mom lifts her out and places her gently wherever Mom wants her. When a little boy learns to ride his bike, he pedals wherever Dad, running alongside, directs him. Children are easily led by their parents because they are utterly dependent on them. We all know how unappealing children who defy their parents are!

That childlike attitude of submission is the humility God is after in each of us. While age may have taught us much about living and making decisions, the spiritually mature understand that they will never know it all. God is seeking people who readily acknowledge what they do not know and who are willing to faithfully walk with God, who does know. This childlike faith helps us stay focused on the hand that is leading us and keeps us from getting sidetracked by distractions.

Overcoming Distraction

Understandably, distractions can throw us off professionally. If you get caught up in office gossip or power struggles, you can neglect to perform your own work with excellence. However, Kingdom workers in the marketplace also need to remember that the day-to-day routine can distract them from the eternal work God has given them to do. At one point in my career, I was caught up with the implementation of a new business plan in my company. I was absolutely swamped trying to meet deadlines. As a task-oriented person, I see days in terms of windows of opportunity. Given the enormity of the task at hand, I felt I could not afford to let a single opportunity for productivity pass. So I spent very little time paying attention to the people in my company.

As it turned out, a great number of my co-workers were facing personal challenges. I felt so overwhelmed by my responsibilities that I did not hear the silent cries of my colleagues for help—until the Holy Spirit tugged on my heart. Two of my colleagues were facing tremendous health issues; one of them had become critically ill. Another co-worker was struggling with the tragic death of a teenage friend in a car crash.

When I learned of these situations and realized that I had near-ly missed opportunities to share the Gospel, I repented and asked God to forgive me. I repented for failing to see the obvious pain on my co-workers' faces. I repented for not being accessible to the people to whom God had sent me. I also repented for failing to spend the necessary time in prayer for my workplace and col-leagues. Then I began to listen attentively to God as He led me to minister in different ways to each person. Sharing hope and salvation with my co-workers did not prevent me from fulfilling my duties. I just needed to glance in that side-view mirror spiri-tually and make a quick adjustment.

Staying Focused During Trials

I used to laugh when I heard some of the older saints in my church say, "Higher level, bigger devil." When you are an entry-level employee, you tend to believe the opposite. You believe that the higher you ascend in management, the easier the work will be. But let me tell you from experience that those old saints were right! Each new level of responsibility—spiritually or pro-fessionally—makes life much more complicated, and at every new level, hearing and seeing the will of God requires a greater level of attention. Each new marketplace assignment affords us an opportunity for greater dependence on God, both to help us fulfill our professional responsibilities and to carry His Gospel to the lost.

One of the hardest times to maintain your focus on God is when you face opposition or conflict. Be encouraged! God has not left you defenseless. He has given you the strategy for your walk with Him and your warfare in the places He has appointed you. Your relationship with Christ Jesus allows you to put on

God's armor—which translates into God's character, His nature, His protection and His purpose (see Ephesians 6:10–19). When you are armed with His protection, He will enable you to stay focused on the eternal while you walk through the temporary challenges.

I mentioned that your race and gender are part of the special qualities God has given you to fulfill His purposes. That means challenges that arise as a result of these qualities only serve to propel us to our destiny. I remember once when the executive director of our company retained the services of a consultant to help with strategic planning. In preparation for this process, the consultant was expected to meet with all line staff and managers. She kept a list with the names of all staff, position titles, length of employment and educational backgrounds that she could refer to as she met with each of us.

> God has given us the strategy for our walk and our warfare in the marketplace.

I happened to be the only manager in the office early one morning when the consultant approached me for an interview. After a few introductory remarks about her goals and background, she began. As we went through her basic questions, she stopped me several times with comments and questions such as, "You speak so well, not that Black talk!" "Where did you grow up?" "You're not like the others." "Your family must have money." Obviously fueled by unfavorable stereotypes of Black people, she made no attempt to hide her astonishment at my competence and posture. (It is not uncommon for me to refer to myself and my race as both "Black" and "African-American" in written and verbal communications. However, throughout this particular exchange with Charlotte, I purposefully chose to use "Black" to accentuate her comment about Black talk.)

I never responded to her comments or questions directly during the course of our question-and-answer period, but I did so afterward. As we wrapped up the interview, I told her I wanted to share some important information with her before she approached the remaining staff. I knew from our brief time together that she would likely offend the nearly 40 percent of the staff who represented racial minorities.

"Charlotte, I know you have deadlines and a lot of work to complete, but you are heading for a major blowup with some of the staff," I said. "Please give me a few minutes to explain what I mean."

She was willing to hear me out, so I went on. "I know you did not intend your extra comments and questions regarding my racial background to be offensive, but they give the impression that you think most Black people are low achievers and poorly educated. I am a good judge of people, and based on what you told me about yourself, you mean well. You need to understand that Black people are as diverse in education, socioeconomic status and so on as they are in skin color. Some of us were blessed with the opportunity to earn college degrees; others did not have that opportunity or chose not to go to college. Your surprise at meeting a Black person who is well-spoken, successful and in a responsible position will be perceived as insensitive, divisive and racist among our staff."

"I'm sorry. It wasn't my intent to offend anyone," Charlotte apologized. "I didn't understand it before now, but maybe I was responding to what I had heard about the verbal skills of most Black people. I wanted to compliment you, but it just didn't come out that way."

"Charlotte, I understand," I smiled. "That's why I wanted to take the time to talk with you so that you don't find yourself in an explosive situation later down the road. We can all learn a lot from each other, and being open and honest is just one way to start the dialogue."

In the days ahead, Charlotte and I did begin a regular dialogue about her interviews, the responses she got and the strategic company plan. We also talked about our faith in God. By the time Charlotte left, we had begun a friendship that spanned several years. It was not until her father became ill and she moved to another state to take care of him that we lost contact. But I continue to think fondly of Charlotte, the growth in our relationship and our shared faith in God, which transcended perceived barriers. The experience with her taught me the importance of fixing our focus on our eternal purpose in the face of a temporary challenge. God had protected my heart with His breastplate of righteousness, so Charlotte's insensitive comments did not offend me. Instead, I could reach out and minister to her as He intended. This helped my sister in the Lord become more effective professionally and in her service to Him.

> God can use race and gender to propel us to our destiny and to help us witness to others.

God's grace is more than sufficient to help each of us overcome every trial, storm or challenge. Whatever happens in this life, you must deliberately and purposefully accept the specific charge God has given you. You must possess an absolute assurance that God is able to perform His work through you, and you must reflect on your instructions from the Father.

There may be times when you need to fall on your face and pray for a fresh revelation about your assignment. You may have to overlook an offense, as I did. You may have to scan through your prayer journal to revisit the last time the Lord revealed something to you regarding your marketplace assignment. It may even help if you find some uplifting Christian music that will edify you as you navigate the challenges before you.

Just keep reminding yourself that there is no failure in God and that He is eternally faithful and true. Remember that the King of kings has selected you for an important work here on earth. You have been formed and fitted with the capacity to receive instructions directly from Almighty God and to be a vessel that carries His presence. Now walk focused on Him, with confidence that your success has been ordained before the foundation of the earth.

The next chapter highlights the importance of letting our conduct and character represent the One who sends us into the marketplace. We will also talk about submitting to God's authority and also to the authority of His delegates, whoever and wherever they may be (God rules through delegated authority). We will find out how these qualities help us overcome challenges in the workplace and how we can sustain our faith when challenges arise.

Equipping Prayer

Heavenly Father, I am truly thankful for my job and for the ability to serve You in the marketplace. Forgive me for failing to share Your love with people who are different from me. Help me use my spiritual eyes to see all people as You see them. In the marvelous name of Jesus I pray, Amen.

Marketplace Memory Scripture

I will praise the Lord, who counsels me; even at night my heart instructs me.

Psalm 16:7

Marketplace Experience Self-Evaluation

Record a time when you reacted in a stereotypical manner to the gender or race of a boss or co-worker.

Based on the teaching in chapter 4, list one biblical principle you could have applied to that situation.

When do you find it hardest to walk with God?

What steps are you willing to take to keep your vision and hearing fixed on God?

Based on the teaching in chapter 4, rate your new skill level at taking Jesus to work and living out your faith on the job:

    ___ 1.   A Little Better Prepared
    ___ 2.   Much Better Prepared
    ___ 3.   Equipped

Note: *To increase your skill level after your initial reading of the chapter, please pray for wisdom according to James 1:5 and read the chapter again.*

5

Who Do People Say That I Am?

The Reverend Pines was in a bind. He had been in full-time ministry for years, but the congregation no longer brought in enough funds to pay his salary. He needed to take a full-time job in addition to his pastoral duties. After searching the want ads for a couple weeks, he found a position that seemed to suit him. God showed Himself faithful as always, and he got the job.

Unfortunately, Pastor Pines never chose to tell anyone at his new job that he was a minister. He had been out of the secular workforce for so long that he was afraid of not fitting in. This particular office had plenty of sin to confront: cursing, a couple of adulterous affairs, Friday night trips to the bar and visits to the strip clubs, just to name a few. Although this behavior horrified him, his silence gave the impression that he condoned it, or at least that it did not bother him too much.

Months passed, and his compromise began to take its toll. First, he seemed to lose his authority in the church setting. Instead of raising his place of work to the standard of the Kingdom, he was lowering his church ministry to the standard of the world. Over the next months, he seemed to lose the anointing to minister, and he was relieved of more and more of his ministerial duties. Lastly, he became ineffective in his secular job as well. His performance reviews went from good to poor. Unfortunately, he and his family (whom I knew well) ended up leaving their church for another part of the country, never to be heard from again.

If you are a Christian in the workforce, your call to live out your faith at work is not optional. Although it met an important need by supplementing his ministerial income, Pastor Pines saw his secular job solely as an obstacle to his ministry, not as an opportunity for ministry. He did not heed the call to take Jesus to work. Although there is a price to pay for serving the Lord in any context, the price of disobedience is much, much higher.

PRAYER POINT: Pray for knowledge of the character of God.

Heavenly Father, thank You for revealing Yourself to me in ways that challenge me to live a godly life. Please guide me so that I will learn how to acknowledge You in all that I do. In the name of Jesus I pray, Amen.

God's Reputation

"When Jesus came to the region of Caesarea Philippi, he asked his disciples, 'Who do people say the Son of Man is?'" (Matthew 16:13). Jesus did not often ask His disciples to focus on what other people thought of them. After all, many of His exhortations urged them (and us) to focus on what God thinks and forget the rest of the world. He taught that if you go to a house and its inhabitants reject you, you shake the dust off your feet

and move on (see Matthew 10:14). He taught that if you fast to impress people, you are missing the point (see Matthew 6:16). Yet here is Jesus asking His disciples to tell Him who people say that He is. Why should Jesus care what others think of Him?

He does not care, except for one important point: What others think of Jesus will determine their eternal destiny. Today Jesus no longer walks the earth in bodily form, but He sends us as His ambassadors to continue the work of reconciling the world to Him (see 2 Corinthians 5:20). So who men say we are, as His representatives in the marketplace, will be directly correlated to who they say He is.

> What others think of Jesus will determine their eternal destiny.

Remember how Jesus showed who He was? He spent time teaching and training, but also eating and living with His disciples. They watched Him experience joy and sadness and behave with generosity and compassion. Through the life Jesus lived on earth, His disciples learned the character and nature of God.

That is why Jesus told His disciples, *"Anyone who has seen me has seen the Father"* (John 14:9).

> The character and nature of God are what others should see when they see us.

It is easy to identify children by their parents. "Hey, isn't that John's son?" "Oh, you must be Kelly's daughter!" And truthfully, if John's son is rude and disrespectful, we cannot help but see John in a different light. On the other hand, if Kelly's daughter is full of smiles and helps without being told, Kelly's stock goes up. Nothing less is true of how our conduct in front of unbelievers influences their opinion of our heavenly Father.

The character of God should be readily visible in us as we work in the marketplace. This is easy, of course, when we start the day with a great devotional time and our calendar is full of tasks we love. On days like that, we head out feeling confident. But the rubber meets the road, so to speak, when the deadline for the proposal is in three hours, when our division is over budget or when the CEO is coming for a visit. When circumstances tempt us to compromise, distort the truth or engage in other unscrupulous behavior, we must fight for our testimony. We must sacrifice the easy road in order to represent Jesus with integrity. Unless you and I are willing to do this, there will be no difference between unbelievers and us.

We also must experience no confusion regarding what Jesus would actually do in our place. We must know the character of God. Consider for a moment the job titles meted out in the typical work environment. Believers receive a position title just like everyone else, a title intended to reflect the work they are to perform. Your position title designates your professional role. Spoken and unspoken expectations also accompany your title, many of which relate more subtly to the status associated with your position. The key to remember is that, above all else, God has His own expectations of His children. It really does not matter whether you are an executive or the janitor—your status as a believer trumps all.

One man I know has an enormous impact within his area of influence for Christ. James is not the CEO of a large corporation; he is a gas station attendant. His status as a believer does trump all, and he effectively carries out his mission right where he is—even to the general public, not just to his co-workers. For years, we have gassed up at the local station where James works. You cannot miss the place. Christian music streams out of the speakers on the lot, and a weekly Bible verse is pasted on the white Plexiglas window where you pay for your gas. Also obviously visible is a small New Testament Bible leaning against the window with an invitation to purchase it.

James is no stranger to the community. Besides his physical appearance—you cannot help but notice his shiny bald head and his wide smile as he greets customers—the station where he works boasts some of the cheapest gas prices in town. Remarkably, the costs are kept low because only cash payments are accepted. So even people who are not Christian music fans are drawn to the place because of the low gas prices. And with each trip to the gas station, customers receive a dose of the Gospel.

James also openly shares the Gospel with his customers. "One time a woman came in who was shaken up and in tears," he told me. "She came for gas, and she left with gas and Jesus because I shared the Gospel with her!" He also described instances when things did not go so well. "Some customers get angry or offended when I talk about Jesus. Sometimes I just don't seem to reach them, but that doesn't stop me from trying!"

> The status of "believer" is much higher than any other status acquired in the marketplace.

As James spoke about ministering on the job, I sensed his resilient spirit and knew he would not be deterred by rejection or intimidation. Although he has touched many lives through sharing the Gospel, he does not know for certain how many people have accepted Jesus Christ as a result. Yet he remains resolute in his determination to live out his faith in his workplace—planting or watering seeds because he is Christ's representative on his job. Christian ministry is and always will be his number one priority there.

If you grew up in a house like mine, you know that often your parents set a higher standard for you than the school or the teacher did. It might not matter if the teacher said your handwriting was neat enough if Mom said it was not. If you got in trouble and were sent to the principal's office, there was probably a bigger punishment waiting when you got home to tell your dad. In the same manner, God expects to see His children reflect His standard, no matter what expectations are associated with our titles.

Success and favor offer as much temptation for compromise as those discouraging temporary assignments we dislike. In the Old Testament, four young Israelites were sought out by the Babylonian king for their talents and abilities. Once he brought them into his household, he changed their names to fit in with their new Babylonian peers. Daniel was given the name of Belteshazzar, Hananiah was renamed Shadrach, Mishael was Meshach and Azariah was Abednego (see Daniel 1). Neither their name changes nor their enviable position in the king's court changed their faithfulness to God. Unlike Pastor Pines, they knew God had allowed their kidnapping and entrance into secular service for His glory. They always remembered who God made them to be—unlike many Christians who obtain a modicum of success or power in the secular world, then forget what they are really called there for. That was not the case with these four young men. Before long, everyone in Babylon knew about the God of Israel through the character they displayed, which was literally tested by fire.

The character of the One you represent must be the standard for your behavior. No one can be one of Jesus' sheep if he or she behaves like a wolf. This means we do not attack unbelievers in their sin; we offer them truth, hope and a way of escape. The more time we spend studying God's Word and praying, the more prepared we are to live out our relationship with Him in the marketplace. Like the Hebrew boys in Babylon, we are on display for the Kingdom. Like them, we were born to stand out wherever we are so that unbelievers will learn about our God. If unbelievers see Christians as approachable, particularly in their times of need, they will begin to see God the same way.

The Value of Authority

It is impossible to demonstrate God's character to others without demonstrating a healthy respect for and submission to authority. We must accept that God rules through delegated authority—it is He who ultimately puts one person up and puts another down (see Psalm 75:6–7).

I remember one opportunity I had to demonstrate submission to authority under pressure. During my work as an executive with an internationally known organization, I was promoted twice over five years. With each promotion, I encountered a higher-level supervisor who was literally under demonic influence. I was harassed, humiliated and tormented on almost a daily basis. One supervisor made a point of belittling me in the public hallway in front of my staff. To say I was under pressure is an understatement. I regularly retreated to the bathroom *to cry, to pray, to cry and to pray.*

God gave me the strength to stand, though. From day one, I refused to gossip about my supervisor with anyone. I just kept doing my job as unto the Lord. My staff and others marveled at how I kept a respectful attitude toward her as I continued to perform my work diligently. My response ended up having such an impact on others that they began coming to me for prayer and advice. I know that because of my respectful attitude toward authority, I had far more opportunities to witness to the people around me than I would have if I had handled the trial differently.

I also learned how to pray earnestly and faithfully about my marketplace assignment: *Father, bless my supervisor and cause her to do "good" to me, whether she wants to or not. Lord, I thank You for preserving me and keeping me in this place, until such time as You move my supervisor or move me.* I prayed that same prayer for both supervisors. God moved the first supervisor out of that job and that organization. In the case of the second supervisor, God moved me on to a different job.

> We honor God when we respond in a Christlike manner to His delegated authority.

God places a high value on authority because He created it. He is the absolute source of authority in the earth, and He delegates His authority to others who rule:

> *Everyone must submit himself to the governing authorities, for there is no authority except that which God has established. The authorities that exist have been established by God. Consequently, he who rebels against the authority is rebelling against what God has instituted, and those who do so will bring judgment on themselves.*
>
> Romans 13:1–2

Your employer or supervisor is one of those subordinate authorities who represents God's delegated authority at work (see Colossians 3:22; 1 Peter 2:18). Jesus Himself showed submission to authority all of His life (see 1 Peter 2:21–23; 3:18; 4:1, 13). You honor God in your work when you respond in a Christlike manner to His delegated authority. Yet to consistently respond to your employer or supervisor in a manner pleasing to God, you must seek God for revelation about your employer or supervisor and the role in which he or she has been placed. God knows He has placed imperfect people in authority, but that fact often catches us off guard. When you think about it, however, it is amazing that Almighty God can use us and others in spite of our weaknesses and that He delights to do just that.

God often uses delegated authority to help us mature. He can use the most challenging bosses to motivate us toward patience and perseverance. He can use our subordinates to expose weaknesses in us that need development. Watchman Nee makes an interesting observation about authority in his book *Authority and Submission*:

> Before Paul realized authority, he wanted to eradicate the church from the earth. But after he met the Lord on the way to Damascus, he realized that it was difficult to kick against the goads (God's authority) with his feet (man's energy). He immediately fell down, acknowledged Jesus as Lord, and submitted to the instruction of Ananias in Damascus. Paul met God's authority. At his conversion, Paul was brought not only into a realization of God's salvation, but also into a realization of God's authority.
>
> Paul was an intelligent and capable man, while Ananias was a very insignificant, small brother. . . . This shows us that anyone who has met authority will deal with the authority alone; he will not deal with the person involved. We should only think of the authority, not of the person, because our submission is not to a person but to God's authority in that person.

Using Delegated Authority

As a believer, you will also experience opportunities in the marketplace where others are required to submit to your leadership. How you "rule" in these situations should also reflect the character of God. In one company, our receptionist, Marcia, had trouble recording phone messages accurately. My executive assistant was Marcia's supervisor and was the first to bring the problem to my attention. As I have shared, I am very task oriented, so receiving inaccurate or late messages can really throw off my day. Yet I decided to take my time and pray about the situation to see how I might handle it wisely.

The next day at work, I invited Marcia to join me in my office for a chat. During this informal time of sharing, Marcia told me about some of her interests and skills that no one in the company knew she had. When I learned about her creative gifts, I asked her to design an invitation that I could use for an upcoming special event with some of our VIPs. She excitedly took on the task and created the most beautiful invitation I had ever seen anyone produce without specialized software. With her own colored pencils, she hand-drew the detail that the computer was unable to capture.

I began to meet frequently with Marcia, and I learned that in addition to her artistic talents, she was also an adult with dyslexia. She shared with me her impossible dream to work in design or graphics. I shared with her some of the impossible things God had allowed me to do that no one ever thought possible for me—including me.

Only faith in God will enable us to do what God wants us to do and be what He has ordained us to be.

As I continued to pray for Marcia, God showed me strategies for utilizing her gifts. I assigned Marcia different creative tasks that would showcase her unique talents. She created personal birthday cards for the employees in the company, developed flyers and put together volunteer recognition gifts. She even beautified my office with some specially designed knickknacks. Soon we worked together to ensure that whenever she created something, we would place a duplicate or photo of it in a portfolio binder. With every task, Marcia's confidence level increased, and she began to get excited about her next project. After the binder became full, I convinced Marcia that the time was coming for her to "leave the nest." Her relationship with the Lord had grown to a point that she understood He was developing her gifts so that she could be fruitful in another environment. Marcia eventually left the company to become an assistant to a graphic artist. I was honored that God used me to nurture her gifts as part of His plan for her life.

By Faith

We must remember that we can never obtain the character of God in our own righteousness. We will never be able to submit to God and His delegated authorities with only our own willpower. Only faith in God enables us to do what God wants us to do and be what He has ordained us to be. When you rise each day, a portion of your prayer time should be devoted to expressing your faith in God: *Father, I thank You that You are faithful. I thank You that You order my steps and that my faith is enlarged because I have great and high expectations of You. Send me where You want to send me, Lord, and I will do whatever You ask me to do and speak whatever You ask me to speak. In the precious name of Jesus, Amen.*

At midday and intermittently during the day, pray a prayer of thanks for God's sustaining power through faith. Before going to sleep at night, pray something such as, *Father, I commit to You in faith everything that has been done this day. And I commit to You in faith those things that are yet to be done. And Lord God, because of my faith in You, I know that You are fixing those things that I messed up this day. In Jesus' name, Amen.*

Noah had great faith in God. Genesis chapters 6–9 tell his story. He was 480 years old when God instructed him to build the Ark, and it took him 120 years to accomplish it. He was 600 years old when the Flood came. Noah remained faithful in his assignment. And let's not forget that while he was building the Ark, which was obviously time-consuming, Noah had to attend to Mrs. Noah and his sons. He also managed to preach a continuous message of repentance to the bystanders.

Noah's faith was fixed on completing God's assignment. Interestingly, Noah lived another 350 years after the Flood began, so he died at the age of 950. He was already into middle age (or what was then considered middle age) when God told him to build the Ark, and he committed and invested almost an eighth of his entire life to doing so.

With a little imagination, we can compare what Noah experienced to what many middle-aged people face today. He probably contended with physical changes like the rest of us—perhaps thinning hair, weight gain, diminishing eyesight and problems with his knees. Yet he also

There is never an excuse to refuse God's call.

dealt with the ridicule, rejection and scorn of those who watched him building the Ark in a landlocked area for 120 years!

No doubt Noah could have come up with 101 excuses for refusing to cooperate with God's plan. Yet he understood—and you and I must understand, too—that there is never an excuse to refuse God's call. Unlike Noah, you and I have the Bible, with all its instructions, promises and accounts of God's faithfulness. You and I have the Holy Spirit to fill us with power and lead us into all truth. God is expecting a return on His investment in us. Noah had faith in God. We, too, must have faith in God.

Faith is the key to growth both personally and professionally. As early as second grade, my teachers singled me out as a gifted student and public speaker. They gave me opportunities to speak in front of others and represent my school at special events. Then the attacks began. My peers taunted and teased me to the point where I stopped speaking publicly altogether. I rarely even spoke in social situations. This lasted until high school, when I was one of the students selected to represent my school on *It's Academic*, an academic game show competition between high schools that still airs on NBC. On the show, I caught the attention of some local NBC executives, who asked if I would be in some of their commercials. I agreed, and the barrage of attacks I had experienced in elementary school started a second time. Again, I gave in to the tormentors and quit speaking in public unless required. This continued through college and into my early career years.

For several years, I was comfortable in my self-pity. I hid behind the mask of being a "quiet person." One day while I was in prayer, the Lord showed me that if I wanted to walk in complete liberty in Him and if I wanted to fulfill His plan and purpose for my life, I must have total faith in Him. Then the Lord brought to my mind the following passage of Scripture:

> *Before I formed thee in the belly I knew thee; and before thou camest forth out of the womb I sanctified thee, and I ordained thee a prophet unto the nations. Then said I, Ah, Lord God! behold, I cannot speak: for I am a child. But the Lord said unto me, Say not, I am a child: for thou shalt go to all that I shall send thee, and whatsoever I command thee thou shalt speak. Be not afraid of their faces: for I am with thee to deliver thee, saith the Lord.*

> Jeremiah 1:5–8, KJV

God made it clear to me that whatsoever He told me to speak, I should speak. I must not fear the faces of people because He would deliver me. After years of being paralyzed by what others thought, I experienced the Lord's deliverance. The fear that had dampened my effectiveness for Jesus melted away as I surrendered to Him in faith. Now when I speak, I tap into the power of God, reaching beyond my own abilities. The object of my faith has made it all possible for me, as He can for you in whatever He calls you to do.

As I walked with God, I learned to cast my cares on Him because He cares for me (see 1 Peter 5:7) and to lean on Him when I felt weak. *"But they that wait upon the Lord shall renew their strength; they shall mount up with wings as eagles; they shall run, and not be weary; and they shall walk, and not faint"* (Isaiah 40:31, KJV).

You can learn to cast your cares on Him and lean on Him, too, as you walk out His call for you in the marketplace. Remember, your identification with Christ comes with a commitment to a faith-filled life. Sovereign God has already walked every place that your journey in the marketplace will take you.

Now, begin to see yourself as the missionary in the marketplace that God has called you to be. Walk believing in your heart and mind that with God's purpose and provisions, you have the grace and the favor to complete your assignment. Walk with the assurance and readiness to fulfill God's mandate for you, which I will talk more about in the next chapter.

Equipping Prayer

Father God, thank You for helping me to discern with all wisdom and understanding seasons and opportunities without timidity or fear. Let me bear fruit in every work that my hand undertakes, to Your glory and honor. Father, please help me remember that it is all about You and not about me. I am an instrument of Your purpose. Please help me walk in the fullness of Your power and might.

Now, Father, I thank You that from this day forth I will walk in a greater measure of faith. I will speak only those things that generate more faith. I will do only those things that are faithful in Your sight. I will think only those thoughts that will multiply my faith in You. Thank you for Your faithfulness and each and every provision You have made for me—not only those I see now, but those yet to come. I praise You and thank You in the awesome name of Jesus, Amen.

Marketplace Memory Scripture

I will lie down and sleep in peace, for you alone, O Lord, make me dwell in safety.

Psalm 4:8

Marketplace Experience Self-Evaluation

Record a time when you operated in fear rather than faith in the marketplace.

Based on the teaching in chapter 5, list one biblical principle you could have applied to that situation.

How does the realization that "it is not about you" change your perspective about your purpose?

What are some practical ways that a faith in God can help Christians become more effective in their marketplace assignments?

Based on the teaching in chapter 5, rate your new skill level at taking Jesus to work and living out your faith on the job:

    ____ 1.   A Little Better Prepared
    ____ 2.   Much Better Prepared
    ____ 3.   Equipped

Note: *To increase your skill level after your initial reading of the chapter, please pray for wisdom according to James 1:5 and read the chapter again.*

6

Search-and-Rescue Mission

In late August 2005, all America watched in horror as Hurricane Katrina made landfall on the Gulf Coast, with deadly results. With billions of dollars in property damage and nearly 2,000 lives lost, it was easy to forget that the Coast Guard rescued more than 33,500 people in the midst of the catastrophe (see http://www.uscg.mil). For days on end, the brave men and women of the Coast Guard worked round the clock to rescue the perishing. They operated from helicopters and boats, with insufficient equipment and on very little sleep, to seek and save those who were in danger of drowning or dying of thirst.

When crises strike us at work (thankfully on a much smaller scale), it is also easy for us to focus on the damage and forget the search-and-rescue mission at hand. God wants us to remember that behind that bleak sales report, that accounting disaster or that missing inventory are the lives of people—people who are drowning without Him and dying of thirst. Jesus promised He could provide the living water that would eternally satisfy the thirstiest souls (see John 4). As God's vessels in the marketplace, it is our job to seek out those souls. Even in the midst of a crisis, we must work tirelessly to deliver the living water to those in desperate need.

Committed to Holiness

Light shines brightest through a clear vessel, and living water is best served from a clean glass. As He leads us in our marketplace search-and-rescue mission, God wants us to be holy vessels so that what He pours through us will be pure. We stand as His representatives who have been entrusted with a message of righteousness, hope and salvation. When we live the holy lifestyle God has established, we will naturally separate ourselves from the world's attitudes, ideas and inclinations as we trust in Him—our ultimate example of holiness. God made it clear from the beginning that He expects us to be holy in all of our ways:

PRAYER POINT: Pray for knowledge to evangelize and disciple others.

Heavenly Father, I thank You for the grace to lead others to You through a word, a deed or a smile. Help me not to forget the mercy that You extended to me when I first came to You. In Jesus' name I pray, Amen.

> *Speak to the entire assembly of Israel and say to them, "Be holy because I, the Lord your God, am holy."*
> Leviticus 19:2

> *Therefore, I urge you, brothers, in view of God's mercy, to offer your bodies as living sacrifices, holy and pleasing to God—this is your spiritual act of worship.*
> Romans 12:1

Since we have these promises, dear friends, let us purify our-selves from everything that contaminates body and spirit, per-fecting holiness out of reverence for God.

2 Corinthians 7:1

Put on the new self, created to be like God in true righteousness and holiness.

Ephesians 4:24

Since everything will be destroyed in this way, what kind of peo-ple ought you to be? You ought to live holy and godly lives.

2 Peter 3:11

Everyone who has this hope in him purifies himself, just as he is pure.

1 John 3:3

What does holiness look like in the marketplace? Does it mean that we are cold or stuck-up and we keep to ourselves? Absolutely not! It means that the presence of God we carry brings an inex-plicable sense of conviction to those around us. We cannot res-cue people if we look as though we are drowning, too! Not only do we reject the coarse jokes or rude language of our co-workers, but our presence in the room will bring such behavior to a stop. Our holy lifestyle and standard should be so powerful that we do not even have to speak a word to change the spiritual environment in the break room or boardroom. Yet we are far from being aloof around others; our humility makes the Holy Spirit free to work through us.

> We cannot rescue people if we look as though we are drowning, too!

How do we obtain this kind of holiness? God tests and tries us to increase our capacity for holiness, our submission to the Holy Spirit and our ability to divide the flesh from the spirit. When we experience trials at work, we must first conduct an honest self-evaluation to see where we may be responsible for our own difficulties. Once our consciences are clear, we can be sure that these tests will help us serve God's purposes more effectively.

I once went through a phase when my marketplace leadership was disastrous, as well as being a major disappointment to God. At the time, I was a strict disciplinarian, an insular decision maker and an aloof leader full of self-righteousness and a critical spirit. Yet the God of all mercy dealt with my unrighteousness not according to the full merit of my sins, but through a series of difficulties on the job that allowed me to see the error of my ways. I was faced with several concurrent and potentially devastating marketplace crises—multiple staff resignations, bleak financial forecasts coupled

> Whatever is not advancing the purposes of God is probably hindering them.

with a terrible cash flow, employee morale issues and competitor threats to our market share. As I began to examine myself, pray and repent, I sought deliverance and was rescued by Almighty God, who looked beyond my faults to address my biggest needs.

Today, I can honestly report that the godly lessons I learned during that phase of my career saved my workplace, saved my job (and those of many others) and forged changes in my work style and lifestyle. And now on a daily basis, I ask the Holy Spirit to temper my tongue, to shape my character and to transform me into the missionary in the marketplace God wants me to be. Admittedly, I continue to make mistakes, but I am quick to repent and to try to model the good qualities I am sharing with you. It is my heart's desire, as it should be of every believer in the marketplace, to earnestly live a life that is pleasing to God.

When we become holy, we move beyond knowing about God and start partnering with Him to expand His Kingdom. Sometimes this expansion means tearing down the works of the enemy; sometimes it means building up the works of God. As Solomon said, "To *every thing there is a season, and a time to every purpose under the heaven. . . . A time to kill, and a time to heal; a time to break down, and a time to build up"* (Ecclesiastes 3:1, 3, KJV).

In the marketplace, we can look at the "time to break down" Solomon referred to as stopping whatever is unproductive. I mean primarily our Kingdom productivity here, not productivity in the natural. Whatever is not advancing the purposes of God is probably hindering them. We need to tear down the unproductive things in our lives to see God's search-and-rescue mission fulfilled through us. What if the members of the Coast Guard had concerned themselves with media coverage during Hurricane Katrina instead of focusing on the task at hand? That would have been unproductive given their task and training, and thousands more lives might have been lost. We do not want to lose people spiritually because we forsake our Kingdom task and training to focus on unproductive things.

We must also never compromise God's standards in our pursuit of excellent job performance. Work-oriented activities that seem productive in the natural may in reality be immoral, unethical or even perverse. In the eyes of the world, such activities are sometimes mislabeled as excellent business practices. For example, financially profitable ventures in the workplace often continue unabated, whatever their moral or ethical faults. The fact that they are profitable justifies them in the eyes of some who do not hold to God's standards. Yet Almighty God sets standards so much higher than our reasoning and comprehension. We must ask God for divine discernment and draw a line in the sand, so to speak, in our workplace. Then we must steadfastly refuse to compromise, trusting Him completely to make up for any temporary losses we may suffer on the job while we pursue holiness. The cleaner we are inside, the brighter His light will shine through us in our places of employment.

A God of Second Chances

Even as you strive to let your light shine before men (see Matthew 5:16), you will also have ample opportunities to observe the frailty of others. Often, the greater your authority at work, the greater the risk such people pose to your career. I remember one particular search-and-rescue mission of mine when I was CEO of a company. It involved a man I will call Jacob. Jacob had stumbled big-time. He had lost his prestigious position with a large company because of accusations regarding financial mismanagement and improper conduct with another employee. Out of concern for their company's reputation, the executives had decided to dismiss him quietly without filing formal charges.

When I met Jacob, he had not worked for several months in the wake of the scandal. His family was on the verge of losing their home and everything they owned, and no one would hire him because of his blemished past. Although Jacob had repented, made a public confession of his sins at his church and begun counseling, he remained a broken man whose circumstances were worsening daily. During our first meeting, Jacob spoke about his repentance and his desire to begin his life anew.

Although he had followed biblical principles regarding spiritual restoration, he needed some practical help right away. He needed a job!

I spent a significant amount of time in prayer for Jacob until I obtained what I believed was an answer from God. I contacted Jacob and told him I was willing to help him if he was really serious about starting over. He reiterated his desire to do whatever was necessary. Well aware that his high-risk status could put me at risk, I could only justify employing such a person by insisting that he apply for an entry-level job that was otherwise difficult to fill.

Although Jacob formerly had been in a high-ranking position, he humbled himself and accepted my terms of employment. Another of my terms was that Jacob must fully disclose the circumstances of his dismissal from his previous job on his employment application and in the presence of the interviewer. He also had to promise me that he would not betray my trust by repeating his past mistakes or by getting into any other trouble.

Jacob was hired at an hourly rate barely above the minimum wage. As he worked diligently and faithfully in that position, his heart was encouraged, his character was strengthened and he was able to modestly contribute to the needs of his family. His performance was so exceptional that his supervisor gave him outstanding evaluations, which led to merit increases in pay. At the end of two years, Jacob left for a salaried position with a larger company. He disclosed his past situation to his new employer and received an assignment that would not involve managing money or employees, but at last he had the fresh start he needed.

The God of second chances had used me as His marketplace missionary to give Jacob another chance. Through prayer and the application of biblical principles, I was able to help a lost sheep fully return to the fold. Jacob proved the authenticity of his repentance in my company, and then he leveraged that performance to advance his career once again. Through humility and hard work, he once again became the provider and protector his family needed. God changed Jacob's story from hopeless to hopeful, and I was grateful to be part of that search-and-rescue process.

Casting Your Net

When you have been saved for a long time, it is easy to forget how precious the Good News of Jesus Christ is. Yet God puts us in the marketplace to show compassion to those who have not yet found this treasure. Pray that God would help you discern the small but continuous opportunities both to pray for people around you and to celebrate the small things in their lives with them. For instance, on Monday you might approach a co-worker who seems stressed out and pray with him about that special meeting he has or that project he is working on. Later in the week, you might let him know that you were thinking about him and prayed for his family. Little things like this plant seeds of God's truth and love and let people know you care.

God reminds us in Hebrews 3:13 to *"encourage one another daily."* A word of encouragement can do wonders. An act of love and kindness can turn someone's life around. God will give you wisdom and guidance about how to approach each person. Think of each interaction with co-workers in terms of the Holy Spirit drawing them closer to Him. You may not see

> Pray that God would help you discern the small but continuous opportunities both to pray for people around you and to celebrate the small things in their lives with them.

your "catch" completely on board yet, but you can rest assured that God is using your obedience through the process as a crucial part of His search-and-rescue mission in your workplace.

Speaking with Power

Just as a vocational missionary labors in prayer over the group he or she is reaching, marketplace missionaries must do the same. Take time each morning to seek God's wisdom and anointing. Ask Him for direction regarding the people He wants you to encourage. Ask Him how to effectively minister to them, and ask Him for the right words to say and the courage to say them.

To be encouragers and speak with power, you and I must tame our tongues. I have seen more Christians than I care to remember compromise their effectiveness because of loose lips and idle chatter. The Bible exhorts us,

> *Likewise the tongue is a small part of the body, but it makes great boasts. Consider what a great forest is set on fire by a small spark. The tongue also is a fire, a world of evil among the parts of the body. It corrupts the whole person, sets the whole course of his life on fire, and is itself set on fire by hell. All kinds of animals, birds, reptiles and creatures of the sea are being tamed and have been tamed by man, but no man can tame the tongue. It is a restless evil, full of deadly poison. With the tongue we praise our Lord and Father, and with it we curse men, who have been made in God's likeness. Out of the same mouth come praise and cursing. My brothers, this should not be.*

> James 3:5–10

How did Jesus tame His tongue? He only said what He heard His Father say. As search-and-rescue workers for the Kingdom, we must let God speak through us, too, and take time to affirm others while resisting the temptation to criticize them. We must learn how to build up and edify them—while rejecting any participation in office gossip. And we must always be ready to pray.

> Prayer may be the most spiritual thing we can do, but it is no excuse to steal time from our employers.

Not long ago, the Lord prompted me to pray for one particular woman I will call Susan. She was a highly paid, respected and seasoned corporate executive working on a couple of projects for me. Although I was Susan's supervisor in this instance, she had decades of executive experience that far exceeded my own, and she was regarded as incredibly intelligent in her field. The Lord used the nature of our work projects, however, to place me in a position relative to her that provided me with a unique opportunity to reach out to her.

In response to the Lord, I approached Susan to ask if I could pray for her—but I did it during a mutual break time so that we would not be stealing time from our company. Prayer may be the most spiritual thing we can do, but it is no excuse to steal time from our employers. As I emphasized earlier, God expects us to work diligently and responsibly as good stewards of the job, title, salary and responsibilities entrusted to us.

Susan and I sat down at the table in an empty room that smelled faintly like that morning's coffee. As I prayed for Susan, I felt the warmth and electricity of the Holy Spirit entering our midst. We were both surprised when I began to sob. I was overwhelmed by a sense of grief and anxiety for her, and I began to detect in my spirit that she was very ill. I decided to ask her about any health challenges she might be facing. She was shocked! She had been wracked by fear and uncertainty for weeks, but had been careful not to share her condition with anyone at work. She began to sob as well and told me that her breast cancer had returned. Although we were both weeping, I sensed her tremendous relief at being able to share this heavy burden with another person.

We prayed a bit more, and when our break ended, we dried our eyes and returned to work. A few days later, I knew the Lord wanted me to talk to her about salvation. We met to pray during our lunch break, and God allowed me to lead Susan to Christ. Needless to say, we both rejoiced along with the hosts of heaven!

Perhaps you will have a wonderful opportunity to lead a co-worker to Christ, as I did. Here is a simple prayer like the one I used with Susan—you can print it on a Post-it note or index card to keep on hand in your purse, your wallet or your briefcase: *Dear Jesus, I believe in You. I believe that You are the Son of God. I believe that You died for my sins and rose from the dead. I repent of my sins and accept Your forgiveness of them. I confess that I accept You now as my Lord and Savior. Thank You for coming into my heart and taking complete control of my life. Thank You for filling me with Your Holy Spirit. Thank You for Your amazing love. In Jesus' name I pray, Amen.* (If you have not yet accepted Jesus as your Lord, take a moment now to pray that prayer yourself. Then you can begin to take Jesus to work with you and learn how to live out your faith and your life for Him.)

A few months after Susan accepted the Lord, I returned from my summer vacation to learn that Susan's husband had a brain tumor. Anxious about the effect of such a huge challenge on a new believer, I immediately sought her out and told her I would pray for her husband. Her response surprised me. She said that a nurse at the hospital had prayed for him, and Susan had asked the nurse if she was connected with me. I did not know the nurse, but I was amazed that Susan immediately connected the Light she saw in the nurse with the Light she saw in me. That nurse, too, understood her call as a Kingdom search-and-rescue worker on the job and responded to this couple in tremendous need. At this writing, Susan and her husband are still fighting toward complete healing, but Susan now has Jesus to depend on and her eternal destiny is secure.

No Apologies, No Regrets

Even as God moves us with tremendous compassion for those around us, we must remember that we need not apologize for our faith. Jesus Himself never apologized for the Gospel or for how difficult it could be for some people to give up everything and follow Him. Consider Peter's exhortation:

Who is going to harm you if you are eager to do good? But even if you should suffer for what is right, you are blessed. "Do not fear what they fear; do not be frightened." But in your hearts set apart Christ as Lord. Always be prepared to give an answer to everyone who asks you to give the reason for the hope that you have. But do this with gentleness and respect, keeping a clear conscience, so that those who speak maliciously against your good behavior in Christ may be ashamed of their slander. It is better, if it is God's will, to suffer for doing good than for doing evil.

1 Peter 3:13–17

We must never forget that the world resists being confronted by the reality of our convictions. What is familiar spiritually to us can seem strange and even frightening to them. Even those who understand the Gospel may be bound to an ungodly lifestyle that they know they will have to forsake. That is why it is so important that we can clearly articulate why we believe what we believe. It is also important to demonstrate that only an intimate relationship with Christ Jesus as Lord and Savior will bring consistent fulfillment and meaning to anyone's life.

> Jesus never apologized for the Gospel.

By bearing the fruit of the Spirit, we can nourish the souls of unbelievers and backslidden believers alike and draw them to the Lord.

Of course, not everyone will be excited about hearing our message or our testimony. We may be mocked or even despised, just as our Lord was while He walked the earth. Despite such rejection, though, never lose heart. While rejection may feel like a personal attack, most people are simply antagonistic to the God we serve. And if we allow Him to direct our paths, we can also confidently depend on Him to redeem every interaction—even those that seem negative at the time they occur.

> Some people in need of rescue will reject our efforts simply because they are not yet thirsty enough.

Some people in need of rescue will reject our efforts on their behalf simply because they are not yet thirsty enough. Jesus said in John 7:37 that anyone who was thirsty could come to Him and drink. In the life of an unbeliever or backslider, a thirsty moment may occur in the midst of a crisis. It is up to us to be watchful and ready when those moments occur. Jacob, the man I helped, would probably have been far less receptive to the ministry he needed before he was let go from his initial job. Likewise, God used the tragedy of Susan's illness and later her husband's illness to minister to both of them through me and through the nurse.

Many times, however, someone whom you pray with in a crisis may move away from you when the crisis passes and go back into their worldly ways. Do not be discouraged when this happens. Continue to plant your seeds. A family friend of ours, Officer Elliott, has to do just that, yet he never gives up.

"The workplace can be a highly antagonistic environment for Christian officers because most of their co-workers are not saved," Officer Elliott told me. "There are all the pressures and demands that trip some officers up, but most just enjoy sinning."

I listened attentively as he talked about his interactions with fellow police officers and his law enforcement work. He spoke in generalities until he mentioned Officer Wilson. During a crime scene investigation, Elliott noticed that Wilson, his assigned partner for that day, appeared distracted. They had worked together on occasion but knew little about each other's personal lives. Yet Elliott, who continuously prays for guidance on the job, sensed that God was leading him to ask Wilson what was going on.

When time allowed, Elliott followed through on what he had been sensing from the Lord and learned that Wilson was facing a major family crisis. Although Wilson's little girl was under a doctor's care, she suffered from a major illness that required divine intervention. After praying for Wilson's little girl, Elliott took another bold step and began to pray for Wilson. Before their prayer time had ended, Elliott led him in the sinner's prayer, and Wilson accepted Jesus Christ as his Savior.

Officer Elliott told me that crises in the personal and professional lives of his fellow officers are often the vehicles that afford him an opportunity to share Jesus. Still, in some instances after the crises have passed, the officers he has reached out to will return to their previous sinful behavior. He continues to minister to them anyway. And each time he shares the Gospel at work, he is risking his job, his reputation and his relationships with other officers on the police force because his marketplace subculture does not embrace God. In spite of that, Elliott willingly works for God in his marketplace because "that's what I'm supposed to do."

Like Officer Elliott, cast your net wide and wait for those windows of time, those thirsty or *kairos* moments, to come again. *Kairos* is an ancient Greek word meaning "the right or opportune moment." It is one of two words the ancient Greeks used for time. The other word, *chronos*, refers to chronological or sequential time, while *kairos* refers to a time in between—an intermediate time when something special happens. In many Christian churches today, *kairos* is used to denote a God-given time that is laden with choice and opportunity.

Kairos moments are special times of visitation when God offers us something miraculous and amazing—if we seize the moment. Just as I had to be obedient in praying for Susan's healing the first time and her salvation the second time, we must always cooperate with God's will and timing to reap the benefits of those *kairos* moments. We will net a much greater catch for the Kingdom if we are sensitive to the Holy Spirit's leading than we will if we preach at people every day until we turn blue!

Fishing for Men

Whom did God send to speak to you or touch your life in your greatest hour of need? You may not recall the details, but no doubt you have a memory—maybe even more than one—of a hand that reached out, a voice that comforted and encouraged, or some other unusual or extraordinary act of love that pointed you to Jesus Christ.

Every day God sends His faithful vessels out on a search-and-rescue mission to fulfill the Great Commission, just as He sent people to rescue you. God knew just what you needed before you joined His family, and He knows just what others need as well. That is why God offered up the ultimate sacrifice of Jesus Christ, so that "whoever believes" would be saved. He loves us that much! As John 3:16 says, *"God so loved the world that he gave his one and only Son, that whoever believes in him shall not perish but have eternal life."* And Hebrews 7:25 tells us Jesus Christ *"is able to save completely those who come to God through him, because he always lives to intercede for them."*

To faithfully fulfill His purposes, God wants us empty of ourselves and full of Him so that we will be available and responsive to His leading. The more we tame our tongues and our flesh, the better suited we are for our Master's use. Peter learned an invaluable lesson about responsiveness at the beginning of his walk with Jesus. Luke chapter 5 relates that after working overtime fishing all night and catching nothing, Peter was ready to call it a day (so to speak). Yet while he washed his nets and readied himself to head home, Jesus came and asked Peter to push out his boat a little, that He might better teach the crowds from it. And when Jesus had finished speaking to the crowd, he said to Peter, *"Put out into deep water, and let down the nets for a catch"* (Luke 5:4).

Such an order at that time of day made no sense, and as a successful

> God can and will give us creative strategies so that we can diligently conduct His Kingdom business while performing our marketplace work with excellence.

fisherman well acquainted with his trade, Peter knew it. He had applied all his skill to the task, but the fish just were not co-operating. But because Jesus said so, Peter did as he was told. He answered Jesus, *"Master, we've worked hard all night and haven't caught anything. But because you say so, I will let down the nets"* (Luke 5:5).

Pride could have prevented Peter from doing as Jesus told him. Yet he did not allow his credentials, his experience or his reputation to prevent him from responding to the call of God. And look what happened as a result of his obedience: *"When they had done so, they caught such a large number of fish that their nets began to break. So they signaled their partners in the other boat to come and help them, and they came and filled both boats so full that they began to sink"* (Luke 5:6–7). By following the Master's instructions to lower his nets, Peter received an amazing and abundant catch—two boatloads full!

Will you let your credentials, experience or reputation prevent you from accomplishing the Kingdom work God has ordained for you in the marketplace? Or will you obey—even when a word from God does not immediately make sense to you—and net an amazing and abundant catch, as Peter did?

St. Francis of Assisi is often quoted as saying, "Preach the Gospel; if necessary, use words." God can and will give us creative strategies so that we can diligently conduct His Kingdom business while performing our marketplace work with excellence. Our conduct, our attitude and our character can speak volumes about the love of Christ and lay the foundation for our marketplace search-and-rescue mission. With earnest time spent in prayer according to James 1:5, our nets, too, can be filled to overflowing.

Let's move on to examine God's standard for His representatives in the marketplace. In the next chapter, we will discuss various ethical situations where we may need to take a stand of integrity, and we will see how important it is to depend on the Holy Spirit for wisdom and courage.

Equipping Prayer

Father, I thank You for helping me choose to want to reach others in my marketplace. Please help me continue to abide in Your Word so that I will be courageous. Help me continue to spend time in Your presence so that I will receive individualized strategies for each person You send across my path. In the triumphant name of Jesus I pray, Amen.

Marketplace Memory Scripture

A fortune made by a lying tongue is a fleeting vapor and a deadly snare.

Proverbs 21:6

Marketplace Experience Self-Evaluation

Record a time when you interacted with someone at work who was facing a professional or personal crisis.

Based on the teaching in chapter 6, list one biblical principle you could have applied to your encounter with the person.

Why do you think it is harder for some Christians to maintain godliness as they ascend in position, money and power?

Should you be concerned about the morality of others?

Based on the teaching in chapter 6, rate your new skill level at taking Jesus to work and living out your faith on the job:

> ___ 1.   A Little Better Prepared
> ___ 2.   Much Better Prepared
> ___ 3.   Equipped

Note: *To increase your skill level after your initial reading of the chapter, please pray for wisdom according to James 1:5 and read the chapter again.*

7

The Line in the Sand

I can still hear my kindergarten teacher's voice: "Stay within the lines. Lines are our friends!" To clumsy little fingers eager to color the entire page, lines can seem very inconvenient. They can feel like meaningless obstacles to our creative impulses. Yet, as every parent knows, if a child ignores the lines, all she brings home is a big, colorful mess!

Of course, my kindergarten teacher was right. Lines are our friends. Lines define, measure, separate and divide. They let us know what is acceptable and what is not. And just as some children become frustrated with the care and discipline it takes to stay within the lines, some grown-up believers carelessly forsake the boundary lines God has set up for their conduct. This may happen while facing one of life's challenges, or it may happen while surrounded by others who live by a different standard. Unfortunately, it takes only one act of compromise to destroy years of faithfulness in the eyes of those around us. While the Lord understands that we are not perfect, He does not turn a blind

PRAYER POINT: Pray for knowledge to remain holy.

Father God, I want to thank You for the direction You have given me to live a godly life. It is my desire to exhibit thoughts, words and deeds that testify of Your righteousness and holiness. In Jesus' name I pray, Amen.

eye to such compromise. Instead, He offers us the power of the Holy Spirit to enable us to live within His boundary lines.

Standing on His Standard

God is calling you and me as His standard-bearers. According to the American Heritage Dictionary, a standard-bearer is "one who carries a standard or banner, especially of a military unit; an outstanding leader or representative of a movement, organization, or political party." As God's standard-bearers, we must always be found on His side in whatever battles we find ourselves. Instead of a literal flag, we raise up our witness, our work style, our integrity and our purity for others to rally around and follow. Do not be surprised if your standard becomes a point of division among your co-workers, though. After all, Jesus asked, *"Do you think I came to bring peace on earth? No, I tell you, but division"* (Luke 12:51).

When Moses returned to the camp with the Ten Commandments, he found the Israelites had forsaken their relationship with God. Although every one of the Israelites had experienced God's miraculous deliverance from Egypt, confusion reigned in Moses' absence. In light of this rebellion, *"The Lord said to Moses and Aaron, 'Separate yourselves from this assembly so I can put an end to them at once'"* (Numbers 16:20–21). The people of God had to choose: They could not follow the Lord and burn incense to idols. Those who wanted to remain with the Lord had to declare it publicly. As for those who decided God's way was not worth the trouble, *"The earth opened its mouth and swallowed them, with their households and all Korah's men and all their possessions"* (Numbers 16:32).

In today's marketplace, God is drawing the same line in the sand. As His return draws nearer, He is clearly distinguishing those believers who belong to Him from unbelievers and from those who name His name but do not follow His ways. His standard-bearers in the marketplace are to stand on His side of the line as the ones to whom He has entrusted a message of righteousness, hope and salvation. Leviticus 19:2 reminds us, *"Be holy because I, the Lord your God, am holy."* By living the holy lifestyle God has established, these "believer-leaders" will separate themselves from the world's attitudes, ideas and ethics as they, like Moses, follow God's glory.

> By living a holy lifestyle, "believer-leaders" separate themselves from the world's attitudes, ideas and ethics.

As Moses did when he returned from the mountain, there will come times when we must take a stand for God and draw that "line in the sand." Sometimes the circumstances will relate to our personal holiness; other times they will relate to professional integrity. The Bible exhorts us, *"Since we have these promises, dear friends, let us purify ourselves from everything that contaminates body and spirit, perfecting holiness out of reverence for God"* (2 Corinthians 7:1). Praise God that He knows we are a work in progress—many of the times that we are forced to draw a line in the sand actually will be opportunities for us to perfect our holiness in the fear of the Lord.

A Little Leaven

For a period of time, I led a corporate team that set monthly marketing and sales goals for a large tristate area. Among other things, it was my responsibility to ensure that we met those minimum monthly goals. For the most part, we had no problems. To be sure, we struggled at times and had to persevere through some dry spells, but my team members were hardworking and responsive to my leadership.

Then a man I will call Stan joined our group. Intelligent, charming and energetic, he seemed like the perfect addition to our team of achievers. He certainly talked like someone who could get the job done, and everyone enjoyed his company, including me. His winsome demeanor made it all the more surprising that he failed to make his quota for two consecutive months. If a team member thought he or she would be unable to make the monthly goal, I was supposed to be notified ahead of time so I could offer suggestions and encouragement. Stan never came to me for help; I only found out he had issues when the numbers came in.

Without the conviction of the Holy Spirit and the stand of righteous people, all kinds of evil will continue as long as they are financially profitable.

After several meetings between us to discuss his performance and the company's policy regarding sales goal achievement, I warned Stan he had one more chance to get it right. He gave me a self-deprecating smile and promised I would not be disappointed. When the third month's numbers came in, I discovered that not only had Stan failed to meet his goal, but he had actually lost the previous month's clients. I knew this was the last straw.

We met to discuss termination plans. As usual, Stan accepted my criticisms with grace, then he proceeded to tell me about the new home he had just purchased and other serious financial obligations that he was on the verge of wrapping up. Before I knew it, I caved in and gave him yet another chance.

Ironically, the problem was no longer just Stan. The mood of the entire staff shifted. Within days, the initiative and drive that made my team one of the highest performing in the company began to wane. Nearly everyone's numbers began to fall noticeably. Next, I began to get wind of grumbling against my leadership and the company in general. Suspicious that people were discouraged about my decision to go easy on Stan, I was shocked to learn that most of the complaints could be traced back to him! I had spared his job out of a sense of compassion, and now he had the nerve to stir up trouble.

I learned firsthand the truth of Paul's statement, *"A little yeast works through the whole batch of dough"* (Galatians 5:9). Stan's lax attitude, disguised by charm, had infected my entire staff. I prayed and then took immediate action to correct my mistake. I terminated Stan and worked with the remaining team to rebuild goal performance and to repair our relationship and trust. I drew the line in the sand, albeit a little late, and the Lord honored my stand.

Building Up, Breaking Down

Remember that God has already planned to bring His righteousness to the earth. As we follow His direction, He will instruct us on how, when and where to draw the lines in the sand. Do not be surprised if your actions shake things up. Sometimes your stand will build something up; other times it will tear something down.

As Solomon once said, "To *every thing there is a season, and a time to every purpose under the heaven. . . . A time to kill, and a time to heal; a time to break down, and a time to build up"* (Ecclesiastes 3:1, 3, KJV).

The "time to break down" that Solomon refers to often occurs when the Lord decides to halt something that is not producing Kingdom results. It is not unusual for a venture to appear prosperous by the world's standards but be plagued internally by immorality or corruption. Without the conviction of the Holy Spirit and the stand of righteous people, all kinds of evil will continue as long as they are financially profitable. That is why God is calling so many of His people as living epistles in the marketplace who will hear His voice and raise His standard.

At your leisure, please read the following Scriptures for biblical examples of God choosing a specific time to break down what man built or attempted to build in his flesh: Genesis 11:1–9; Genesis 19:24–25, 28; Joshua 6:20; and 2 Corinthians 10:4–5. When you read these examples of what the Lord breaks down, you will note that the obstacles stand for a period of time before He does so. If you see a stronghold of unrighteousness that seems impregnable, do not be discouraged. When God says it is time for it to fall, just be ready to do your part.

Solomon also told us there was a "time to build up," a time to fortify or build anew. God wants us to separate ourselves from unbelievers because He wants to show the world that His presence and favor rest upon us. As we pursue His holiness, He wants to build up His Kingdom in us. Here are the tangible things the Lord will build up as we act as standard-bearers of His righteousness:

1. *The Church.* How can God build His Church while we are at work? As we edify other believers in the marketplace

and serve as an example to them, we build His Church. *"And I tell you that you are Peter, and on this rock I will build my church, and the gates of Hades will not overcome it"* (Matthew 16:18).

2. *Our Relationship with Christ.* The more we stand for Him, the closer we become to God. Just as a couple's marriage is strengthened by all they have been through together, our relationship with our Savior grows deeper as we walk through life's challenges with Him.

> *So then, just as you received Christ Jesus as Lord, continue to live in him, rooted and built up in him, strengthened in the faith as you were taught, and overflowing with thankfulness.*
>
> Colossians 2:6–7.

3. *Our Faith.* The more we take a stand for God, the more we are forced to trust Him. Like a weight trainer adding more and more resistance to his workout, we build up our faith as we face down unrighteousness.

> *But you, dear friends, build yourselves up in your most holy faith and pray in the Holy Spirit. Keep yourselves in God's love as you wait for the mercy of our Lord Jesus Christ to bring you to eternal life. Be merciful to those who doubt; snatch others from the fire and save them; to others show mercy, mixed with fear—hating even the clothing stained by corrupted flesh. To him who is able to keep you from falling and to present you before his glorious presence without fault and with great joy—to the only God our Savior be glory, majesty, power and authority, through Jesus Christ our Lord, before all ages, now and forevermore! Amen.*
>
> Jude 20–25

4. *Other People.* The others around us, unbelievers included, actually benefit when we take a stand for God. As His blessings come in response to our stand, everyone around us is blessed as well. Consider the following three translations of Proverbs 29:2:

> *When the righteous are in authority, the people rejoice (KJV).*
>
> *When the righteous are increased, the people rejoice (ASV).*
>
> *When the righteous thrive, the people rejoice (NIV).*

Now, the fact that some people will rejoice does not mean that everyone will. True righteousness frequently provokes mixed reactions at best. Some people will respect us for our integrity, and others will likely resent us because our conduct has raised the standards or pricked their consciences. God wants us to behave the same whether 90 percent of the people are with us or whether we must stand alone.

Standing for Personal Holiness

At one time in my career, I wondered if I was a "creep magnet." I had the same unpleasant experience in two very different work settings: Male supervisors blatantly solicited me for an adulterous affair. I examined my behavior thoroughly and knew that nothing in my conduct or communication could have led them to believe that I was interested or that I was even that type of person. Yet both men made entirely inappropriate advances.

In both cases, I learned from female co-workers that these men viewed me as the "fresh meat" in the office. I responded to this information by trying everything I could to get my supervisors to stop their inappropriate advances. I appealed to any sense of morality they might have, I threatened to report them to the authorities and finally I announced that I would quit my job if the advances continued. In both instances, they stopped harassing me upon learning that I was ready to resign. I learned how to take a stand politely but firmly.

> We must manage work by not letting it become an idol and by raising God's standard there.

Naturally, it was hard to respect these two supervisors afterward, but I continued to do my work as unto the Lord. A short time later in my tenure with the second company, I learned something strange. The supervisor who had harassed me there confessed he was secretly proud that I had resisted his advances, unlike so many other women. I discovered what many women know—that some unbelievers view such exploits as a sport. It is like sparring with a foe or playing a hunting game. Although this man had little personal morality to speak of, he was moved in a positive way by the fact that I did not compromise God's standard.

Serving Idols

God condemns idolatry countless times in the Bible, declaring, *"Do not follow other gods, the gods of the peoples around you"* (Deuteronomy 6:14). Time and time again, He called His prophets to draw the line in the sand over the issue of idolatry. When we think of worshiping idols, we tend to imagine burning incense in front of a statue or sacrificing an animal. Yet I contend that anything for which we harbor inordinate affection becomes a god to us.

Work itself becomes an idol if we give it the dominion over our lives that should belong only to God. It is not wrong for us to enjoy our work or its benefits. Solomon declared, *"When God gives any man wealth and possessions, and enables him to enjoy them, to accept his lot and be happy in his work—this is a gift of God"* (Ecclesiastes 5:19). Yet we must never forget that we are to manage our work, not the other way around. When we let our work manage us, either unwittingly or out of our own selfish ambition, then we are in danger of falling into idolatry. If the Holy Spirit convicts us that this is the case, we must *"put to death, therefore, whatever belongs to your earthly nature: sexual immorality, impurity, lust, evil desires and greed, which is idolatry"* (Colossians 3:5).

How can we discern whether we are giving work the appropriate place in our lives or whether it has become an idol? How do we know if our career is shaping our spiritual goals instead of being shaped by them? First, we must recognize when we become preoccupied with work. If we are thinking about work during worship time, or if we are weighed down by our responsibilities even on the weekends, we need to reexamine our mental priorities.

> Intimacy with God is not reserved for the spiritually perfect; it is for the spiritually hungry.

The next step is to take an honest look at how we make decisions. When we discover that we are asking God to bless our work goals instead of continually submitting all our goals to Him, work is on its way to becoming an idol in our lives. Ultimately, when we find our self-esteem and our sense of purpose wrapped up in our careers more than in Christ Jesus, work has become a god to us.

Idols are rivals for our affection, and they try to steal our intimacy with God. Knowing God personally is the ultimate goal of every Christian, and our work only has meaning as we subordinate it to the goal of knowing Him more. Sporadic devotions instead of consistent prayer time hinder our ability to effectively communicate with God. Therefore, we must jealously guard the time the Lord gives us to spend with Him and use that time to submit everything in our lives back to Him.

Intimacy with God is not reserved for the spiritually perfect; it is for the spiritually hungry. Spiritually hungry Christians will do whatever it takes to keep their hearts right before the Lord. They allow nothing to distract them from communion with God. Every Christian must recommit him- or herself to this kind of life on a daily basis.

Those three Hebrew boys—Shadrach, Meshach and Abednego—drew a line in the sand against idolatry. They refused to worship anyone but God alone. God expects nothing less from you and me. When the boys left the fiery furnace, they were unscathed—their hair was not singed, their clothes had not changed and there was no residual smoke from the furnace on their bodies or clothes. This public fiery furnace experience demonstrated to all the unbelievers that God keeps those who belong to Him and rewards their faithfulness. The boys were promoted in the same palace where they had encountered their fiery trial.

As He did through the three Hebrew boys, God intends to astonish those around us through our testimony. The marketplace has its versions of the fiery furnace, too: demotion, reprimand, suspension or termination. Because Jesus was with them in the fire, no harm came to the Hebrew boys. We are to remain faithful to God, as they did, whether He chooses to deliver us before we enter the fiery furnace, during or after. No matter what we encounter, our conduct is to reflect a holy, righteous and uncompromised work style and lifestyle.

Drawing a line in the sand will often require that we separate ourselves from the popular wisdom of the day. To preserve our testimonies and faith, we must fight vigilantly against any internal tendencies toward duality and double-mindedness. Yet each time we take a stand, we will find that God trusts us with greater responsibility and will move us to higher places of authority for our good and His glory.

> Drawing a line in the sand will often require separation from the popular wisdom of the day.

God desires to prosper His servants with godly success and to make them channels of blessings to others. In the next chapter, we will see how the trials God allows are linked with good success and are used to draw unbelievers to God.

Equipping Prayer

Holy God, as I do my part to help set the captives free, please keep me mindful that I am Your standard-bearer in the marketplace. With every move I make, please continue to teach me to draw strength from You so that I will not grow weary. In the holy name of Jesus I pray, Amen.

Marketplace Memory Scripture

The Lord will grant that the enemies who rise up against you will be defeated before you. They will come at you from one direction but flee from you in seven.

Deuteronomy 28:7

Marketplace Experience Self-Evaluation

Record a time when you had to choose whether or not to make a public "righteous stand" on your job and draw a line in the sand.

Based on the teaching in chapter 7, list one biblical principle you could have applied to your situation.

How does a lust for human glory conflict with glory for God?

How do you die daily to the flesh and live out a transformed life in the midst of conflict and turmoil?

Based on the teaching in chapter 7, rate your new skill level at taking Jesus to work and living out your faith on the job:

___ 1.   A Little Better Prepared
___ 2.   Much Better Prepared
___ 3.   Equipped

Note: *To increase your skill level after your initial reading of the chapter, please pray for wisdom according to James 1:5 and read the chapter again.*

8

Good, Godly Success

This book of the law shall not depart out of thy mouth; but thou shalt meditate therein day and night, that thou mayest observe to do according to all that is written therein: for then thou shalt make thy way prosperous, and then thou shalt have good success.

Joshua 1:8, KJV

Early in my career, I read that powerful verse from Joshua and wondered if there could be any other kind of success besides "good success." Over the years I have learned that there is another kind. Godly success—the "good success" God promises us if we keep His Law in our mouths, minds and hearts—makes us prosperous, but it also makes us channels of blessing for others. Worldly success, on the other hand, may glitter on the outside with possessions and power, but it is devoid of peace.

Outward success is fleeting. At most, it will last for the decades during which we walk this earth and perhaps provide our heirs with a good start or even a luxurious lifestyle. Yet more often than not, it disappears a lot faster than that. That is why so many business leaders lie awake at night worried sick about the competition. God's workers in the marketplace rest well, knowing that only God can grant us good, godly success, and only God allows us to keep it. Yet this peace does not translate into complacency. As with any other goal, we must pursue professional success in order to achieve it. We simply recognize along the way that the creativity, energy, talent and work ethic that enable us to succeed all come from God.

As God's missionaries in the marketplace, we also need to understand that our success is not just for us. God uses our blessings to bless others and attract them to our leadership. Perhaps God is calling you to start a business that will employ other Christians so that they, too, can prosper. Maybe He is promoting you to an executive position so you can be instrumental in ushering your company into a new level of innovation. When we begin to see our success from the perspective of how it can bless others around us, we will find that God sends other Christians into our midst to support the work He is doing through us.

Deborah was this kind of marketplace missionary. She was a judge with exceptional leadership skills and wisdom, and was highly respected by all Israel. Despite her good reputation and the demand upon her gifts, Deborah focused on serving her followers rather than lording it over them. She used godly wisdom

PRAYER POINT: Pray for knowledge to remain holy.

Heavenly Father, please sound an alarm in my spirit and speak to me directly or through Your prophets and intercessors when I am about to wander from the faith in pursuit of success. Help me to pursue holiness in all that I do. In Jesus' name I pray, Amen.

to exhort and encourage others such as Barak to succeed. Barak was an army commander, commissioned by God.

Deborah, a prophetess, the wife of Lappidoth, was leading Israel at that time. She held court under the Palm of Deborah between Ramah and Bethel in the hill country of Ephraim, and the Israelites came to her to have their disputes decided. She sent for Barak son of Abinoam from Kedesh in Naphtali and said to him, "The Lord, the God of Israel, commands you: 'Go, take with you ten thousand men of Naphtali and Zebulun and lead the way to Mount Tabor. I will lure Sisera, the commander of Jabin's army, with his chariots and his troops to the Kishon River and give him into your hands.'"

Barak said to her, "If you go with me, I will go; but if you don't go with me, I won't go."

"Very well," Deborah said, "I will go with you. But because of the way you are going about this, the honor will not be yours, for the Lord will hand Sisera over to a woman." So Deborah went with Barak to Kedesh.

Judges 4:4–9

In the male-dominated society of the ancient world, Deborah understood that she could wield her remarkable position of authority as a woman to bless those around her. The Bible tells us that after talking with Deborah, Barak went on to rout Jabin's army, and Israel was victorious! Deborah spoke in a straightforward manner without using her feminine charm to manipulate people. God's path to good success will be characterized by integrity and honorable communication. The Bible exhorts us to speak the truth in love (see Ephesians 4:15). We must never fall into the enemy's trap of speaking deceptively flattering words to preserve our jobs, manipulate a situation or get ahead. Of course, we exercise wisdom and discretion in our words, but we do it, as Deborah did, for the Lord's honor.

Where Is Your Treasure?

We all say that money cannot buy happiness, but sometimes it sure seems as if it might buy something pretty close. I once knew some people who had every material possession they could possibly want: multiple vacation homes, chauffeur-driven limousines, the most expensive clothes and jewelry and an expansive portfolio of investments and holdings. They had everything except Jesus Christ in their lives.

Despite having obtained every possible measure of worldly success, their hearts were broken. A loved one was struck with a debilitating disease. They hired the best doctors to treat him and even funded the best scientists to search for a cure, all to no avail. In the midst of this unthinkable tragedy, they had no true friends to rely on who would offer comfort and share their grief. Their life of luxury had decayed into a life of torment.

Desperately they threw themselves back into the business world, buying companies, restructuring them and selling them again. Dominating the lives of other people, for good or ill, seemed to bring them closest to the happiness and satisfaction they craved. I attempted several times to share the Good News of Jesus Christ with them, and each time I was rebuffed in no uncertain terms. They seemed more content to be miserable with their riches than to invite Jesus, who longed to heal them, into their lives.

> Material success is a side benefit of serving God, not an end in itself.

Jesus taught us, *"But seek first his kingdom and his righteousness, and all these things will be given to you as well"* (Matthew 6:33). We not only have a different focus from unbelievers, but we also respond differently to prosperity. We see God as the giver of every good and perfect gift and as our ultimate source and provider (see Philippians 4:19; James 1:17). This understanding causes us to place material success in its proper context—as a side benefit of serving God, not an end in itself.

Maintaining this godly perspective makes us less likely to compromise our priorities or standards for that business deal or that promotion because we know that doing so would defeat our entire purpose of living and working for God. Since we live in a society obsessed with material possessions, unbelievers tend to measure our success by our wealth, professional status and outward symbols of prosperity. The material success of a Kingdom worker is different, though, because he gives God the glory for it and is willing to sacrifice it for Kingdom priorities. Deuteronomy 8:17–18 reminds us of the ultimate purpose for all our wealth:

> *You may say to yourself, "My power and the strength of my hands have produced this wealth for me." But remember the Lord your God, for it is he who gives you the ability to produce wealth, and so confirms his covenant, which he swore to your forefathers, as it is today.*

God-Sufficiency

Shelves of self-help books tell us that fear is the number one obstacle to success. I believe that fear paralyzes many Christians in the marketplace, preventing them from taking the bold actions that will lead to both ministry and professional achievement. However, the answer to fear is not to believe in yourself more or tell yourself how wonderful you are. The answer is to cultivate a healthy dependence on God. When we cannot imagine making a move or taking a step without hearing from God, then we have arrived at a place I call "God-sufficiency."

Philippians 4:19 declares, *"My God will meet all your needs according to his glorious riches in Christ Jesus."* God wants to be our source not only in times of need but also in times of plenty. We have all seen that huge quarterback who just won the Super Bowl smile into the TV camera and shout, "Hi, Mom!" Along with having their cuts cleaned up and bruises kissed, children long to share their successes with their parents. God wants that kind of affection and reliance from us. Remember, the greater our dependence on God, the greater the power He releases through us.

> Faithfulness in Kingdom matters will result in opportunities to pursue God's mighty work.

Jesus walked a life of total reliance on God and saw God's power unleashed on earth in unprecedented ways. We, too, can acquire this same God-sufficiency as we walk with God's purpose in our hearts.

When you are faithful in Kingdom matters and rely on God for your marching orders, God will cause those in authority over you to show you favor. After four months of prayer, Nehemiah requested a leave of absence from his job as cupbearer to the king so he could go on a Kingdom mission. The king granted his request, and Nehemiah went to Jerusalem as a governor to rebuild the walls and gates around the city (see Nehemiah 2). As God did with Nehemiah, He is still granting His people favor with their leaders, new assignments and leaves of absence to pursue His mighty work.

There are times God simply wants to remind us that He is our source—our job is not. My husband, Wilbert, entered an extensive period of prayer regarding a Kingdom burden God had placed on his heart. God directed him to request a one-year leave of absence from his federal government job to complete ministry study. This leave of absence occurred during a period of reengineering in his department. During his absence, supervisors eliminated many jobs and made large shifts to the overall operating procedures. Yet not only did God preserve Wilbert's job so that he could return twelve months later but He also granted him a significant salary increase. All this occurred while he was elevating his level of ministry service in response to God's leading. This kind of promotion would never have seemed possible in the natural realm. Yet we serve a God who is limitless in power and might. With God directing and ordering our steps, we cannot help but have "good success."

Learning God's Lessons

A person living a life of reliance on God will celebrate not only when the victory is at hand but also in the middle of the storm. We must take comfort in the reality that the trials we face will enable us to fulfill God's destiny for our lives. Trials and challenges can seem like the opposite of success when we are facing them. In reality, trials are just another way God can catapult us to our next stage of godly success.

> Everyone who tries anything will fail at some point—whether or not God's lesson is learned in the midst of it will make the real difference.

There are times, of course, when we face challenges because of our disobedience, but even these times serve to prepare us for greater things. Everyone who tries anything will fail at some point; the difference is whether or not we learn God's lesson in the midst of it. This was brought home to me when a young high school student job-shadowed me for a week.

"Does your staff like you?" she asked. The question startled me and caused me to think. I was literally lost in thought for a couple minutes as I mentally skimmed over my leadership roles. If someone had asked me that same question at a much earlier point in my career, the honest answer would have been, "People either love me or hate me—with most probably hating me." For years, I wielded my authority and righteous indignation so harshly that I was probably closer to a military officer than a manager. I was heavy-handed with rules, regulations and even my faith, both in displaying it and demanding that others accede to it. Under my management, you either shaped up or shipped out. I was quick to discipline or terminate staff—always justifiably, but without compassion. It was either my way or the highway.

What the high school student did not know was that several years earlier, I had been invited to a "heavenly inquisition" of sorts; an encounter with God that caused me to reevaluate how I was representing Him in the marketplace. I had to repent for how I handled the authority He had entrusted to me. While I was experiencing the occasional victories for Christ in the workplace, I was not bearing fruit at the level God intended. After this encounter with Him, I made a conscious effort to be the best representative of Jesus that I could be at work—both in my work standards of excellence and in Christ's standards of righteousness.

To get to this place of transformation, I had to learn how to submit to the authority of God over my life while at work. As I moved as God directed, I saw God heal, restore and bring fruitfulness to many lives. For example, instead of just terminating employees, I helped some workers whose abilities were mismatched with their current positions. I encouraged them to think about new careers or find places of employment for which they were better suited. I do not want to give the impression that I became a soft manager. Quite the contrary—I still held true to my high standards of excellence at work. But I also prayerfully sought God's direction in the details and developed some compassion along the way.

The high school student's question reminded me of how far I had come and how important it was for me to stay the course. I chose not to answer her question directly. I did not want her to misunderstand any answer I would give. Instead, I explained my leadership approach and demonstrated it in front of her for the rest of the week. My prayer was that my confidence and demeanor would give her a picture of someone who seeks to please the God of all mercy, who is also the God of all justice.

> While we may have to deal with natural consequences for our mistakes and failures, God can always use a truly repentant heart as a vessel of honor.

God has used every one of my failures to teach me how to be a better employee and a better manager. With each mistake, I have learned and applied invaluable lessons that have ultimately ushered me into positions of greater responsibility. I wish I could tell you that everyone accepted my flaws and accepted my apologies, but that was not always the case. Praise God that our success is not dependent on our perfection! While we may have to deal with natural consequences for our mistakes and failures, God can always use a truly repentant heart as a vessel of honor.

Many of the trials we face also result from confrontations with powers of darkness. Such situations can feel unbearable, but often we can look back at them to discover that they still served to propel us to our next assignment. The world's way of dealing with conflict is to get the best of someone else before they get the best of you. Yet God prescribes exactly the opposite approach:

"Whatever you do, work at it with all your heart, as working for the Lord, not for men" (Colossians 3:23).

Remember that everyone at work is watching us. They are watching to see how we handle the joys and successes of our labor, as well as our trials and tribulations. Our responses

> People at work are watching to see whether our actions reveal the Kingdom of God or our own flesh.

reveal either the Kingdom of God or our own flesh. We must invest time in God's presence to be renewed so that onlookers can have a clear picture of what God is like as they watch us handle our trials. Remember what Joseph said to his brothers who betrayed him and sold him into slavery? *"You intended to harm me, but God intended it for good to accomplish what is now being done, the saving of many lives"* (Genesis 50:20).

Our goal, particularly when facing trials, should be to accept the purpose behind everything God allows in our lives. In this light, every struggle can become a path to more intimate fellowship with God. Trials develop our character and cause us to lean on God for guidance, wisdom and comfort. Some tribulations actually prepare us for special work God has planned. We learn to work under pressure—to think creatively, to make quick decisions and to respond to insults with compassion and kindness. Saul's persecution of David helped prepare David to become king. When Joseph was sold as a slave and then falsely thrown into prison, it helped prepare him to lead the most powerful empire of his day.

Although we can understand intellectually that challenges will yield the benefits of righteousness, they still hurt. We can make matters worse by spending too much time talking to other people about our problems instead of talking to God. By yielding to

God, we cooperate with His plan for our lives and ultimately follow His lead to our "good success."

Learning to Love

The character God develops in us through trials always postures us for greater success. It is not unusual for these trials to be contained in a single person! God teaches a multitude of lessons through such difficult people. He teaches us how to love and forgive, and He reveals our own character flaws in the process. When learning these lessons at work, we must remember God's standard for our conduct:

> But I tell you who hear me: Love your enemies, do good to those who hate you, bless those who curse you, pray for those who mistreat you. If someone strikes you on one cheek, turn to him the other also. If someone takes your cloak, do not stop him from taking your tunic. Give to everyone who asks you, and if anyone takes what belongs to you, do not demand it back. Do to others as you would have them do to you.
>
> If you love those who love you, what credit is that to you? Even "sinners" love those who love them. And if you do good to those who are good to you, what credit is that to you? Even "sinners" do that. And if you lend to those from whom you expect repayment, what credit is that to you? Even "sinners" lend to "sinners," expecting to be repaid in full. But love your enemies, do good to them, and lend to them without expecting to get anything back. Then your reward will be great, and you will be sons of the Most High, because he is kind to the ungrateful and wicked. Be merciful, just as your Father is merciful.
>
> Luke 6:27–36

Our capacity and desire for godly success is tested by difficult people. How do I love the boss who makes me miserable?

How can I be salt and light when I feel attacked at every turn? Jesus points out that loving someone who loves us back is easy to do. It is the difficult people who really test our character. We need to remember that God has afforded all Christians the supernatural capacity to love people whom the world deems unlovable.

> Effective marketplace evangelism will require us to pray and love beyond our human capacity.

Our determination to love the unlovable is one of the chief ways God demonstrates His power to the world.

The process of loving the unlovable must begin with prayer. The most difficult person can benefit from our prayers for his or her salvation, health, safety and other blessings. And remarkably, as we pray for others, we find that our hearts and minds become more attentive to their needs. Then it is time to give feet to our prayers. Simply stated, the time comes for us to move beyond the spiritual realm and engage with a difficult individual in a tangible, Christ-centered way. This often involves an act of sacrifice as we extend ourselves to that person. We continue to ask God for revelation regarding a need we can meet or a service we can render. Our outreach may end up being something as simple as offering a smile, a word of encouragement or an act of kindness directed his or her way.

One time I remembered the birthday of a woman at work who had the reputation of being a tyrant. I prayed about the gift that God would have me give her, which ended up being a book of poetry. It turned out that she loved books, especially those that she would not normally buy for herself. Knowing her disposition, I left the gift and a card on her desk one afternoon without saying a word, so that I would not force her to acknowledge the present or me.

A few days later, she passed by my office door. For a brief and awkward moment, she struggled to thank me for the gift, then quickly hurried away. "Thank you" was not known as a routine part of her vocabulary, so I was grateful to know that my small gesture had made at least a small impact. That little interaction began the process of plowing the field of her heart.

> When we walk with God, we are able to willingly serve the people we work with and work for.

Sometimes it is amazing what a small act of kindness can plant in someone. Other times, you will find that your actions water a seed already planted in such a person's heart. In still other instances, you may have the precious experience of reaping the fruit of many years of labor when you lead someone to the Lord.

A corresponding transformation also takes place in our own hearts as we extend God's love to others. As we extend ourselves to love beyond our human capacity, Christ in us energizes us in creative and strategic ways of loving. While I may never know on this side of eternity the full effect of one small gesture, I know each time I make one that I have planted a seed. Others may come who will water, but ultimately God will give the increase (see 1 Corinthians 3:6).

The Secret of Success

Our work allows us to serve others, meet our family's needs and exercise our God-given gifts and abilities. We bring glory to God by working industriously and demonstrating His character. This mindset allows us to develop a genuinely God-centered work ethic, which is the key to godly success. The Bible gives an infallible plan for realizing prosperity and happiness in this life: *"Blessed are all who fear the Lord, who walk in his ways. You will eat the fruit of your labor; blessings and prosperity will be yours"* (Psalm 128:1–2).

Walking with God is the secret of success and happiness. As a result of my relationship with God and my dependence on His guidance, I possess a willingness to serve the people I work with and work for. Following God's instructions, I encourage and support them. I personally invest in the lives of others, realizing that God has blessed me so I can be a blessing to others.

Sometimes God will show us an opportunity to bless others outside our own workplace. That occasionally happens to me. People everywhere need encouragement and support. On one shopping trip, I overheard the following tirade:

"I want to see the manager! I want to see the manager *right now!*" an angry woman yelled at a sales associate.

I was in line right behind the woman and did not miss a single word. The sales associate did her best to explain the transaction in question, but it neither appeased nor thwarted the wrath of her customer. The manager was paged, and after a few minutes the matter was resolved. As I moved to the front of the line, I noticed the associate was distraught. She looked somewhat sheepish following her encounter with the irate customer. I smiled and spoke comforting words intended to put her at ease. I commented that she had handled the situation well and that she deserved "hazardous pay." We both laughed, and her countenance changed. She told me her name was Elsie, and I told her mine was Vera.

From that time on, whenever I shopped at that store I made it a point to stop by Elsie's counter and speak with her. Our chats went on for a couple of months, then I began to share a little about my family, my church and the Lord. In return, Elsie began to describe problems with her husband and son. After briefly and discreetly praying for her during one such exchange, I promised to bring her a special gift the next time I visited the store. I prayerfully sought God regarding an appropriate gift to give Elsie and settled on a certain Christian book. I soon purchased the book and carefully arranged it in a beautiful gift bag. Then I made a trip to the store, taking my daughter with me. When Elsie saw us approaching her counter with the beautiful gift bag, almost immediately tears filled her eyes. She could not believe I had made good on my promise to bless her with a special gift. Elsie opened the bag to reveal the book and thanked me for my generosity, noting that she could hardly wait to get home and read it.

As we left the store after making our delivery, my daughter, who was twelve years old at the time, asked me, "Mom, do you really know her? Why did you give her a present?"

"I don't know Elsie well, but God is helping us get to know one another better," I answered. "I gave her a gift because it is a way for me to demonstrate Christ's love to her. She needs to see that." I was grateful to God that I had included my daughter on my errand because it offered her another practical opportunity to learn how to "love others to Christ."

After a few weeks, I returned to the store and learned that not only had Elsie read the book, but she had also left it lying on the coffee table in her living room in hopes that her husband and son would read it. She described a hunger for the Word of God that had been birthed in her life.

"Thank you so much for your generosity and prayers," Elsie told me again. "I don't know how I can ever repay you."

"It will be more than enough for me if you faithfully live for Christ," I assured her. "Be a demonstration of the love of Christ in someone else's life."

The pathway to godly success is paved with giving. I have seen the greatest returns in my own life as I have given my tithes and offerings to my local church. I have sown my time, talent, counsel and other resources, and I have experienced personal and financial prosperity. I have given with the knowledge that God will provide all I need, and He has allowed my storehouse to overflow (see Malachi 3:10). I have also seen God do some amazing things in the lives of believers and unbelievers who have been touched through church outreach efforts. I recognize that my own personal success, whether at work or in life outside work, is wrapped up in the success of the corporate church body in which God has placed me. When the Body of Christ is prospering, so am I.

Unselfish giving pleases God.

Whether we are giving of ourselves at work, at home, at church or in the community, we must give with Jesus' heart. That means we should not give with the expectation of receiving anything in return from the recipients of our gifts. Like many of us, I had to mature in this area over the years. My mother and her mother were both natural givers, and I inherited this disposition from them. As a child, I gave counsel to friends, volunteered in a number of capacities and gave out of my own pocket when I saw someone in need. As the years passed, I found myself secretly growing resentful when I did not receive back in proportion to what I had given. If I had been there for a friend, I expected loyalty in return. If I had given money, I expected finances to be returned to me in some form or fashion. When I did not see the return I expected, I began to feel sorry for myself.

This "stinking thinking" was the enemy at work trying to poison my giving with a subtle sense of entitlement. I learned that I was not being truly generous if I expected anything in return for my sacrifice. As I sought God about why I felt so lousy in this area, He had to renew my mind (see Romans 12:2). He enabled me to shift my focus off myself and my gain so I could see myself as an instrument of His generosity to others.

It was not an overnight transformation—I had to fight daily not to look to people for a return, but to keep my mindset on Jesus as the giver of every good and perfect gift (see James 1:17). It was only many years later that I began to experience the reciprocation of my earlier acts of kindness in a significant way—not from people to whom I had given, but from people whom God assigned to be a blessing to me. Yet as I pen these words today, I am secure in the reality that God does the giving—we are only instruments of His will. I cannot tell you what joy this brings to my heart to give unconditionally, as God has given to me.

I remember making a presentation to a small group of business leaders convened from all over the country for a special meeting. Those present were impressed and asked me to repeat my presentation for the entire national leadership group later that same day. Naturally, I was delighted. As I waited for the larger meeting to begin, two colleagues approached me, apparently having heard the news. I knew from the expressions on their faces that they were not coming to offer congratulations! They told me "people were saying" that I had been unfairly singled out for special privileges.

One benefit of relationship with God is "favor."

After chatting with these two colleagues for a little while, it became obvious they were talking not just about this particular presentation but also about the resources and opportunities afforded to me at other times. I endured their comments with a smile, then withdrew to a room by myself to meditate. As I prayed, I lifted up the complaints of my peers and asked God to forgive me if I had done anything wrong. God responded almost instantly by telling me that what they had said was absolutely true. I was being given preferential treatment—and He called it "favor."

God reminded me that as His daughter, I should expect favor as a benefit of my relationship with Him. I knew then that my job was to maintain a heart of gratitude and always remember that I was feasting on God's blessings—a godly and successful life. I thanked God for this revelation and went forth to complete my assignment. I gave my presentation with full confidence that God had made it all possible and that there was more to come.

No man or woman can ultimately stop the plans God has for His children. We can disqualify ourselves through disobedience, but no one else has the power to block the blessings He wants to give us. If we allow ourselves to become preoccupied with how others treat us, we can miss our opportunities. Yet if we remain tuned in to Him, God will direct our paths: *"Trust in the Lord with all your heart, and lean not on your own understanding; in all your ways acknowledge Him, and He shall direct your paths"* (Proverbs 3:5–6, NKJV).

Walking with God means that we listen to Him, trust Him and submit to His will. As His representatives, we cannot allow pride or unforgiveness to steal our godly success. Neither can we worry about other people's reactions as we walk out His good plans for us. God's blessings and favor are available to them, too, if they will follow His ways. Godly success comes as a by-product of a growing relationship with Jesus Christ. Let's look more closely at this wonderful benefit of knowing Him in the next chapter.

Equipping Prayer

Heavenly Father, if I have profited at the expense of the Gospel, please forgive me. Keep me ever mindful that my role is to point others to You. Help me to do that without thought for personal gain. In the glorious name of Jesus I pray, Amen.

Marketplace Memory Scripture

Peter and the other apostles answered and said: "We ought to obey God rather than men."

Acts 5:29, NKJV

Marketplace Experience Self-Evaluation

Record a time when you had to choose between the pursuit of money and your Kingdom purpose.

Based on the teaching in chapter 8, list one biblical principle you could have applied to your situation.

How do you define the word *success*?

What lessons have you learned about the pursuit of success that you want to pass on to a younger generation?

Based on the teaching in chapter 8, rate your new skill level at taking Jesus to work and living out your faith on the job:

    ___ 1.   A Little Better Prepared
    ___ 2.   Much Better Prepared
    ___ 3.   Equipped

Note: *To increase your skill level after your initial reading of the chapter, please pray for wisdom according to James 1:5 and read the chapter again.*

9

Remembering Your First Love

I will love thee, O Lord, my strength.

Psalm 18:1, KJV

I was blessed to grow up watching the example of family members who were very much in love. Of course as an adolescent, the affectionate glances and tender words I regularly observed between married family members seemed a little silly to me. When I grew up and got married myself, I recognized these examples of marriage for what they were: the beautiful result of labors of love. I realized how diligently my extended family invested in and protected their marriages over the years. They never let their hearts grow cold toward one another, no matter what trials life brought. I learned from their example not only how to care for my own marriage but also how to protect my relationship with the Lord by remembering my First Love.

As a missionary in the marketplace, you will have many opportunities to grow weary and give up. Some days you will feel as if you are looking at a parade of temptations, each vying to pull you away from your First Love. That is why each of us must follow Jesus' example:

> They went to a place called Gethsemane, and Jesus said to his disciples, "Sit here while I pray." He took Peter, James and John along with him, and he began to be deeply distressed and troubled. "My soul is overwhelmed with sorrow to the point of death," he said to them. "Stay here and keep watch."
>
> Going a little farther, he fell to the ground and prayed that if possible the hour might pass from him. "Abba, Father," he said, "everything is possible for you. Take this cup from me. Yet not what I will, but what you will."
>
> Mark 14:32–36

Jesus' suffering overwhelmed Him, yet He persevered because of His love for His Father God. Jesus' love motivated Him to place the Father's will above all else. Although we can never equal His tremendous sacrifice, He allows us innumerable opportunities to demonstrate our love for God by putting His will first.

As in any relationship, the hardships we endure can deplete our love for God if we do not respond correctly. The fact that we are commanded to remain steadfast in our love for Him (see 1 Corinthians 15:58) should remind us that it is possible for our

PRAYER POINT: Pray for knowledge about how to please God first.

Father, as You mold me and shape me in Your service, help me demonstrate my love for You by remaining mindful of the "big picture" You have for Your Kingdom. Please keep me from doing things that are in opposition to Your will. In the name of Jesus I pray, Amen.

> Love for God
> encourages and
> motivates us to
> love others to
> salvation.

love for God to wane or disappear altogether. Sin, if left unchecked, can cause even a tender heart to grow cold and hardened.

During our time at work, we are almost always separated from our spiritual support system (the members of our family and our local church). This can make our work hours the time when we are most vulnerable to the enemy's tactics. If no one else is around to encourage us, it can be challenging to remember our First Love in the midst of a hectic workday. That is why we must always encourage any fellow believers on the job and be open to receiving their encouragement.

I was once hired as CEO by a company's board of directors, and they promptly asked me to restructure everything. The organization lacked internal controls, was short staffed and had a problematic system of accountability. When I began, the board made it clear that they expected immediate results. This required that I make significant changes within my first 90 days on the job and have the entire transition completed within 36 months!

The task before me was overwhelming, and the position was the most demanding I had ever undertaken. I spent long hours at the office under unbelievable pressure, while no one besides God, my family and a couple members of my church knew what I was going through.

Yet sometime during my first year in that position, an amazing thing happened. A young woman who had been with the organization for some time requested a meeting with me to discuss what she termed "an important matter." Though I was exhausted, I cleared time in my schedule to meet with her. She arrived right on time, took a seat and explained that she had been praying earlier in the week and that God had given her a special message for me.

Needless to say, I was pleasantly surprised. After months of putting out marketplace fires, I was overjoyed to meet someone there who was praying, let alone hearing from God for me. The validity of her message was confirmed as she began to tell me things that no one else knew. Then she spoke about the mighty things I would do for the glory of God. Her words encouraged and challenged me. At the end of our time together, she told me that God had given her the assignment of praying for me.

After she left, I pondered what I had heard from her and lifted it all to the Lord in prayer. I thought with wonder about how God touched the heart of this sister in the Lord to pray for me when no one else at work could share my burden. Throughout my years with that company, God continued to send this woman to encourage me during some of the most difficult and trying times.

Loving God above All

He answered: "'Love the Lord your God with all your heart and with all your soul and with all your strength and with all your mind'; and, 'Love your neighbor as yourself.'"

Luke 10:27

What does it mean to love God with all our heart, soul, strength and mind? It means that our affection and devotion must be strong, centered and fixed on God. We must guard our hearts daily so that we do not compromise or grow cold toward God. While God is standing with arms open wide, beckoning us into His presence, many of us choose not to respond. It might seem almost unfathomable that anyone would consciously choose to withhold affection from God, yet unbelievers and even Christians do so when they ignore His invitation.

> One of the greatest challenges any Christian faces is the daily call to love God deeply and persistently.

We are to offer ourselves to God, desire His presence and be content with Him as the center of our lives. Maintaining our priorities so that we keep our First Love first can seem impossible when our workload presses down on us. Yet those are the times when it is most important for us to seek Him.

One of the greatest challenges any Christian faces is the daily call to love God deeply and persistently. God will never assume second place to anyone or anything, including the job with which He blesses us. He wants to be priority number one in our lives, our all in all, and He will do whatever is required to stay in first place. If the "all" that God wants is our job, then we must be willing to give up our job. If it is our title, our prestige, our fame or our money, we must be willing to give them up, too. As I stated earlier, God wants to prosper us. When possessions compete with our affections for Him, however, they become idols and must be removed.

> Our love for God enables us to love others unconditionally.

In actuality, the more we understand that we are utterly dependent on God for everything, the easier it is to keep our priorities straight. After all, whom would you rather serve: the stuff, or the God who owns all the stuff in the world? When we know in our hearts that God holds our future, it is a lot easier to focus on Him.

This understanding gives us the proper perspective for trusting our boss, our co-workers and our subordinates. We realize that none of these people really hold the power to harm or bless us—that power rests with God alone. Our favor and success is not dependent on what they do or say. This frees us to love them as God loves us, no matter how they treat us. The freedom we find in loving others unconditionally keeps us connected to our First Love. The way we love others, after all, directly reflects the way we love Him.

Forgiveness

Love and forgiveness go hand in hand. God expects Christians to walk in a continuous spirit of forgiveness, which is crucial to protecting our First Love. We cannot love God deeply if we harbor unforgiveness in our hearts. This is so important to our heavenly Father that He made it a critical element of the Lord's Prayer: *"Forgive us our debts, as we also have forgiven our debtors"* (Matthew 6:12).

Jesus taught us that God's forgiveness of us is linked with our forgiveness of others. Undeservedly we petition God to forgive our debts, and God desires that we forgive others for their debts against us (see Mark 11:25–26). If we resist forgiveness, the spiritual consequences we reap are astounding. They include bitterness, self-pity, misery and death. There are also physical and mental health consequences associated with harboring unforgiveness. Extended periods of unforgiveness can raise our blood pressure, place us at risk for heart disease and suppress our immune system. Lower levels of joy and contentment have also been associated with an attitude of unforgiveness.

> There are consequences associated with unforgiveness and bitterness.

I knew a Christian woman who, as a result of years of unforgiveness, developed major health problems. She regularly spoke of the wrongs she had suffered and how she could not wait to be rid of the person causing her grief. Numerous brothers and sisters in the Lord tried to convince her that she needed to forgive because they had begun to observe the devastating effects of her attitude. After several years of living this way, the woman died of a stroke. Those who knew her attributed her death to the bitterness she harbored most of her life.

It is vital to forgive and keep on forgiving. Peter once asked Jesus, *"'Lord, how often shall my brother sin against me, and I forgive him? Up to seven times?' Jesus said to him, 'I do not say to you, up to seven times, but up to seventy times seven'"* (Matthew 18:21–22, NKJV).

To truly forgive, we must discipline our tongues, our minds and our hearts to prevent them from replaying past injury or hurt. This does not mean there will never be moments when we remember an injustice. However, we can control what we decide to dwell on. We can choose to actively dwell on only those things that are edifying:

> *For the rest, brethren, whatever is true, whatever is worthy of reverence and is honorable and seemly, whatever is just, whatever is pure, whatever is lovely and lovable, whatever is kind and winsome and gracious, if there is any virtue and excellence, if there is anything worthy of praise, think on and weigh and take account of these things [fix your minds on them].*
>
> Philippians 4:8, AMP

Worship That Loves

God created us to worship Him. Worshiping Him is our ultimate purpose in life. Yet we tend to mentally limit worship to the songs we sing in church or perhaps on our own time. Those who are salt and light in the marketplace remember their First

Love by making everything they do, including work, an act of worship to God. Learning to worship through work leaves us continually open to fresh encounters with God. True worshipers understand that we are to maintain a consistent and ever-active worship life. No time or place should ever be off-limits to a heartfelt expression of worship to God, whether our worship is a barely audible whisper or a loud shout. In *The Heart of Praise*, Pastor Jack Hayford puts it this way:

> Even in the dark times, we must realize the vast power of worship to give our lives meaning and purpose. For one thing, bowing before any god *declares our values*. If we surrender to the lying deity veiled in feelings of despair and aimlessness when they visit us, we will bow before hopelessness exchanging the Almighty God for a lesser god. But worshiping God even amid despair is a way to defy the Adversary and declare our valuing of the good—the best—in life: The Lord! There is no more worthy purpose to praise; no more worthy time for it! In worship, we also *name priorities*. Putting God first enables us to focus on first things—His love, our blessings, our responsibility to others—instead of the temporary feelings of despair. Worship . . . even forms certain expectations so that our worship determines what we will yet discover in our future.

Our busyness at work can sometimes hinder our worship, but it need not do so. Instead of drifting away from God in chaotic or challenging times, we can allow the pressures of work to drive us closer to Him. Worship is the expression of our intimacy with God. We cannot be truly intimate with God without giving voice to our joy.

Intimacy with God can be expressed through worship anywhere—even at work!

The more we spend time pondering His character and nature, the more words of adoration will pour out of our souls to our Lord. Some time ago, I began the process of listing as many descriptive words as I could that would declare who God is to me. Every day for one month, I spent a considerable amount of time praying by using some of my new worship descriptors. My worship time increased in intensity and fervency as a result. Here are 41 of the worship declarations I made to God during that time (this is the kind of list you can keep in your desk at work and glance at throughout the day):

Lord, You Are:

1. Breathtakingly Glorious
2. Unceasingly Magnificent
3. Indescribably Kind
4. Eternally Faithful
5. Uncompromisingly True
6. Amazingly Wonderful
7. Vast in Greatness
8. Completely Perfect
9. Splendiferous, Oh Lord
10. Illustrious, My King
11. Incomprehensibly Brilliant
12. Astoundingly Awesome
13. Matchlessly Beautiful
14. Extraordinarily Thoughtful
15. Remarkably Powerful
16. Incredibly Loving
17. Supremely Sovereign
18. Infinitely Righteous
19. Forever Holy
20. Exceptionally Merciful
21. Perpetually Good
22. My Distinguished Conqueror
23. Abundant in Grace
24. Marvelously Wise
25. My Peace, My Hope and My Joy
26. Everything to Me
27. My Defense and My Strong Tower
28. My Holy Place
29. My Life—You Are My God
30. Triumphantly God
31. My Valiant, Reigning and Ruling King
32. My Unsurpassed Deliverer
33. My Transcendent and Wonderful Savior
34. My Everlasting Father
35. My Shield and My Buckler
36. My Invincible and Unconquerable King
37. My True and Mighty One
38. My Loyal and Divine Friend
39. Excellency Itself
40. My Majestic Father
41. My Masterful Savior

This list is by no means exhaustive. I encourage you to take time to come up with your own list. You can do this during your commute to work, sitting on your bed, in the corner of a crowded cafeteria or in a quiet room. With Psalm 100:4 as your guide, enter God's gates with thanksgiving and His courts with praise. Begin by telling God what you are thankful for: His love, His guidance, the new job you just started. . . . Speak to God about the many things you are personally grateful for, like health, strength, peace, your job, your family and a relationship with Him. Then begin to utter words of praise to God such as, "Lord, You are holy, righteous, mighty, marvelous and awesome." It does not need to be loud; God can hear when you whisper. Before you know it, you will find yourself caught up in His glory.

Remember your First Love by worshiping Him daily. Use some of the worship declarations I shared above or come up with your own, but do it. Loving God enables us to be caught up in His presence and captivated by His Majesty so that we can bless Him with our entire being. After all, we were created for His pleasure.

Discerning Evil

Proverbs 8:13 reminds us, *"To fear the Lord is to hate evil."* My father, Jesse, worked in management with a public transit company and was quite practiced in discerning evil. It was as if he could smell evil a mile away! Not only did his "gift" help him spot potential threats on the job but it also protected his family from harm. Whether it was employees cheating on their time sheets or a shifty salesman trying to pull one over on a family member, no one with evil intent got past Dad.

My mother, Ruth, on the other hand, was just the opposite. She seemed to find the good in people even if it was just a tiny speck. Her belief that everyone had something "redeemable" inside them fit perfectly with her role as a nurse. It was also a wonderful mitigating factor when I was being punished for disobedience. God used my parents' ministry gifts at work and at home.

Ultimately, God allows our marketplace assignment to utilize our natural strengths and develop our weaknesses. This requires that we become wise and disciplined (see Proverbs 1:1–8), which means we must be open to instruction. To stay faithful to our First Love, we must learn to exercise discernment of both good and evil. This enables us to steer clear of the enemy, as well as seize opportunities to evangelize our co-workers and bosses. Romans 12:9 tells us we can accomplish this by loving what is good and hating what is evil. We hate what is evil by waging war against it in the spirit and by shunning evil behavior. We love what is good by modeling righteousness to our co-workers and by sharing and living the Gospel.

26 Marketplace Don'ts

I want to close this chapter with 26 things to avoid as a missionary in the marketplace. This advice covers nearly every area of work and will help you avoid the traps of the enemy and remain faithful to your First Love.

1. Don't dress like the world. While different industries and businesses tend to have a standard for attire in the workplace, you must be sure not to compromise your image as a Christian in order to satisfy those expectations. When in doubt, always err on the side of modesty and restraint (see 1Timothy 2:9).
2. Don't gossip. Remember, "The dog that brings a bone, carries a bone" (see Proverbs 11:13; 20:19; 2 Corinthians 12:20).

3. Don't expect something for nothing. Operate with the mindset that there is always a price (good or bad) to pay for every acquisition (see Luke 14:28).
4. Don't be jealous. Jealousy is a sin that will block your blessings from God (see Proverbs 27:4; Romans 13:13; 1 Corinthians 3:3; 2 Corinthians 12:20).
5. Don't sell out for money, fame, prestige, power or position. You might gain the world, but you will lose your soul (see Matthew 16:26; Mark 8:36; Luke 9:25).
6. Don't engage in any unrighteous conduct (lying, cheating, stealing, promiscuity, etc.). Sin displeases God, robs us of the things God has for us and makes us look like unbelievers (see 1 John 1:8–10; 3:4–10).
7. Don't make major decisions when you are the most vulnerable due to things like fatigue, stress and physiological factors. If you absolutely must make a decision, pray for guidance, review all aspects of the decision and then move out in faith (see Psalm 25:5; Proverbs 1:5; 20:18).
8. Don't lower your standards. We are children of the Most High God (see John 1:12; Romans 8:16–17; Ephesians 5:1; 1 John 3:1; 4:4).
9. Don't straddle the fence. You cannot serve God and the world (see Matthew 4:10; 6:24; Luke 16:13).
10. Don't act as though your Christianity is not important. God is the essence of our very existence (see John 3:21; 1 Corinthians 8:6; 15:45–49; Galatians 2:20.)
11. Don't limit God. Allow God to do whatever He wants in your life to bring more fruit (see Deuteronomy 3:24).
12. Don't backstab and undermine your colleagues. Worldly competitive tactics should never be our calling card (see Matthew 13:22).

13. Don't behave like a victim. We are more than conquerors (see Romans 8:28, 37).
14. Don't put off for tomorrow what you can do today. We must seize every opportunity while it is day (see John 5:17; 9:4).
15. Don't believe that suffering and persecutions are going to triumph. We must remember that no weapon formed against us will prosper (see Psalm 41:11; Isaiah 54:17; 2 Corinthians 2:14).
16. Don't rest in yesterday's successes. The harvest is plenteous, and there is still much work to do (see Matthew 9:37; Luke 10:2; 2 Corinthians 9:10).
17. Don't always be in a rush to leave the office at the end of the day. Our work ethic must exceed that of unbelievers (see Colossians 1:10).
18. Don't wear your feelings on your sleeve. People will attempt to manipulate your emotions if they know they can (see Psalm 42:11; 43:5).
19. Don't act as though the world owes you anything. God, not man, is your source (see Psalm 24:1; Matthew 6:33; 1 Corinthians 10:26; 11:12).
20. Don't whine and complain. Good things should always proceed out of our mouths (see Philippians 2:14; 1 Peter 3:10).
21. Don't walk in fear of man or evil. God has not given us a spirit of fear (see Psalm 23:4; Proverbs 29:25; 2 Timothy 1:7).
22. Don't get stuck on the amount of time you end up spending in a particular position or on a particular task. God's assignment for you in the marketplace may be a long one or a short one. Our trust in God signifies that we believe that He knows what is best for our lives (see Proverbs 3:5; Daniel 2:21).

23. Don't expect everyone to rejoice in your success. Others may want what you have acquired (see 1 John 2:16).
24. Don't underestimate the enemy. The enemy never wants your good (see Proverbs 22:5; Jeremiah 5:26).
25. Don't disrespect your boss. Respect goes along with submission to authority (see Romans 13:1; Hebrews 13:17; 1 Peter 2:13).
26. Don't engage in unscrupulous activities. They are traps that can bring great ruin (see Deuteronomy 25:16; Isaiah 33:15–16; Acts 24:16).

Remember, what we do and what we refuse to do should demonstrate our total and complete love for God—a love that keeps "first things first" and keeps our First Love first. Our next and final chapter summarizes and reinforces the initial rallying cry I presented at the start of this book for Christians to take Jesus to work and live out their faith in the marketplace.

———————— *Equipping Prayer* ————————

Heavenly Father, love of my life and God of my salvation, thank You for drawing me ever closer to You. As a deer pants for water, my heart pants for You and for a greater revelation of You. With a grateful heart and true reverence, I worship You in spirit and in truth. My earnest desire in all that I do at work, at home and at church is to bring You pleasure and to continuously honor and glorify You. Be Thou exalted in my life and in all that I do. In the majestic name of Jesus I pray, Amen.

————————— **Marketplace Memory Scripture** —————————

You are worthy, our Lord and God, to receive glory and honor and power, for you created all things, and by your will they were created and have their being.

Revelation 4:11

Marketplace Experience Self-Evaluation

Record a time when you did not make use of an opportunity to worship God while at work.

Based on the teaching in chapter 9, list one biblical principle you could have applied to your situation.

How do you know God loves you?

What steps are you willing to take to ensure that God is always the number one priority of your life—your First Love?

Based on the teaching in chapter 9, rate your new skill level at taking Jesus to work and living out your faith on the job:

____ 1.   A Little Better Prepared
____ 2.   Much Better Prepared
____ 3.   Equipped

Note: *To increase your skill level after your initial reading of the chapter, please pray for wisdom according to James 1:5 and read the chapter again.*

10

Enduring until the End

Some people love to pick up a new book and turn immediately to the last couple of pages to see how it turns out. Other people like me get so caught up in a television drama that they simply *must* know how it ends. If I do not have time to watch the show, my curiosity often gets the best of me and I ask my husband and children later how the drama turned out. Naturally, they keep me guessing for several minutes until they finally let me in on the ending. This is particularly true of my son, who enjoys watching my facial expressions change as he takes his time unfolding the plot.

Although God leaves us plenty of surprising plot twists in life, He never withholds the ending from us where His promises and provisions are concerned. In fact, God encourages us to read the ending in His Word, memorize it, meditate on it and rejoice in it because He has much in store for those who endure to the end. Solomon reminded us, *"Let us hear the conclusion of the whole matter: Fear God, and keep his commandments: for this is the whole duty of man"* (Ecclesiastes 12:13, KJV).

PRAYER POINT: Pray for knowledge to remain holy.

Heavenly Father, Your Word is truth and life. Help me to live it without compromise, with an eye toward the finish line. In Jesus' name I pray, Amen.

God is sovereign, and nothing will thwart His plan. His people in the marketplace are a vital part of that plan for a large harvest of souls to come into His Kingdom. His plan for each of us will not be hindered as long as we conform to His priorities.

One time, the restructuring of a large corporation resulted in the elimination of my job and the jobs of numerous other people. The CEO had decided that to save the company money, all senior staff whose salaries were above a certain threshold would be laid off. Our positions would then be filled with junior staff who required less pay.

The timing of that job loss could not have been worse for me. I had spent five years with the organization and was about to be fully vested in the retirement plan. In just a few short weeks, I would also attend the graduation ceremony to receive my doctoral degree. Add to that my responsibility for the financial assistance my husband and I were providing to our extended family, and things did not look very good in the natural. Praise God that we walk by faith and not by sight! God had a ram in the bush for me—actually two rams. Almost immediately following the loss of my job, I became a part-time consultant with a prestigious university. Shortly after that, I accepted the position of executive director with another organization.

What appeared to be a setback in the natural (the marketplace) was really a setup (an opportunity) for God's work to be done in and through me. By letting my not-so-promising realities

become God's wonderfully prom-
ising possibilities, the work of the
Kingdom was advanced in me as I
weathered the storm. Without a relationship with God, we will never
have true peace in the storms of the
marketplace. We must submit to

Our co-workers
need to know that
God can grant the
peace to weather
every storm.

Him, obey Him (see James 4:7–8) and desire His truth more
than wealth or power (see 2 Thessalonians 2:10).

As a missionary in the marketplace, God has anointed you
with the power to occupy the territory He has ordained for you.
You have already been enlisted for service and equipped for the
important work at hand. Though this means you must engage in
spiritual warfare, you must also remember the shrewdness that
characterizes the servants of God. God's practical wisdom, com-
bined with a submitted heart, will guarantee that nothing can prevent you from reaching your destiny in Him.

26 Marketplace Do's

I want to offer 26 thoughts to keep in mind as you begin to see
your career as a ministry opportunity. These thoughts incorpo-
rate lessons from each previous chapter.

1. Do let God be God. We must trust and obey God regarding the things He would have us do (see Isaiah 64:8;
   Jeremiah 18:6; Romans 9:21; 2 Peter 1:3).
2. Do be diligent. The diligent hand shall prosper (see
   Proverbs 10:4; 21:5; Hebrews 6:11; 2 Peter 1:10).
3. Do keep God first in all things. By doing so, we acknowledge His preeminence in our lives (see Isaiah 44:6;
   Matthew 5:33; Revelation 2:4; 22:13).

4. Do be discerning. If it seems too good to be true, it usually is (see Proverbs 3:21; Philippians 1:10).
5. Do be discreet about the intimate details of your life. Pray and ask God what He would have you share and with whom. Failing to seek God's guidance might result in the disclosure of personal information that could harm your career and fuel gossip about you (see Proverbs 2:11; 5:2).
6. Do remember the One who brought you favor and success. It is God who gives promotions and wealth (see 1 Samuel 2:7; Psalm 75:5–7; Proverbs 10:22).
7. Do preserve your purity at all costs. In addition to displeasing God, having a "reputation" for sleeping around will ruin your witness and is nearly impossible to shed (see Psalm 1:1–2; 119:2–4).
8. Do be approachable. Unbelievers need to know they can come to you for help (see Luke 6:27–36; Ephesians 4:29).
9. Do take risks. If the Lord leads you to do something, do it (see Proverbs 3:5; Isaiah 40:28).
10. Do pursue excellence in all things. Children of the Most High God should always be pursuing the best (see Psalm 112:5–7; Isaiah 1:19; Philippians 3:14; 4:13).
11. Do give credit where credit is due. It takes a lot of character to let someone else shine (see Luke 6:31; 2 Corinthians 4:2; 8:21; 1 Peter 2:12).
12. Do rejoice in others' successes. God is the giver of every good and perfect gift (see John 13:34; Romans 1:12; James 1:17).
13. Do prepare for every meeting. Review minutes, anticipate the agenda and ask the Holy Spirit to guide you (see Matthew 5:16; Romans 13:3).
14. Do resist negativity. What you hear, think and believe will impact who you are (see Psalm 85:8; Isaiah 26:3, 12; Philippians 4:6–9).

15. Do steer clear of the gray areas. The enemy is playing for keeps. Behaving as if you just might go over to his camp in some areas may end in your destruction (see James 1:8; 4:8).

16. Do reach out to others. God sent us into the marketplace as lights in darkness. We cannot influence other people if we isolate ourselves (see Matthew 28:19–20; John 1:1–18; 3:1–20; 1 Peter 2:9).

17. Do forgive other people's mistakes. We need to learn how to cover one another's nakedness (see Luke 6:37; James 5:16).

18. Do see yourself as a success even when you make mistakes. As we walk with God, He will instruct us so that we can learn from our errors (see Matthew 3:8; 2 Corinthians 7:9–12; Jude 24).

19. Do confide in mature Christians outside your immediate workplace. Select people who are godly, of good reputation, successful in their own rights and candid (see Proverbs 13:20; Hebrews 5:14).

20. Do be an example of Christ Jesus. We are His representatives in the marketplace (see John 13:14–16; 1 Corinthians 11:1; Philippians 3:17).

21. Do remember your purpose. *Purpose* is our code word for our Kingdom marching orders (see Psalm 33:11; 57:2; Proverbs 19:21; Romans 8:28; Philippians 2:13).

22. Do dream big. We serve a big God (see Exodus 15:11; Psalm 66:5; Luke 1:37).

23. Do protect your joy. The enemy realizes that the joy of the Lord brings strength to God's people. That is why the devil spends so much time trying to steal it from us (see Psalm 28:7; Romans 15:13; Galatians 5:22; 1 Thessalonians 5:16).

24. Do remember to help others. We are blessed to be a blessing to those around us (see Proverbs 17:17; Ecclesiastes 4:9–10; Matthew 7:12; Acts 20:35; Galatians 6:10).
25. Do be courageous. Since God resides in us, we are victorious in Jesus' name (see Deuteronomy 31:6; Joshua 1:9).
26. Do pray always. Your co-workers, boss and workplace can be the recipient of the blessings associated with your intercession (see 2 Chronicles 7:14; Isaiah 65:24; Jeremiah 33:3; 1 Thessalonians 5:17).

The Conclusion of the Matter

Your calling in the marketplace has a definitive beginning and end. God has called some of us to an assignment that may span an entire career. For others, a particular assignment may be much shorter. Rather than concern ourselves with the length of our tenure in a particular job, we must learn how to focus our efforts on the end that God has in mind. Just like missionaries working overseas, the time of service in one country or community might vary according to the need, from a few months to a year or several years. It is no different for the believer in the marketplace. Our time on a job, in a career or with an organization is completely orchestrated by the Lord.

> The lives we impact for the Kingdom of God should take precedence over our concerns about length of service on a job or in a position.

Many Christians in the marketplace have endured unnecessary stress because they failed to heed the voice of the Lord regarding the length of their assignment. Sometimes they choose instead to chase empty ambitions of their own; sometimes they even chase their colleagues' ambitions—thinking that securing a job or position a colleague desires will put them on top and bring them happiness and success. Advancement may well be God's plan for us—done His way—but we are called primarily to advance the Kingdom. When we are truly able to perceive our marketplace assignments as opportunities to take Jesus to work and share the Gospel with our co-workers, the days, months or years spent on a job or in a position will be inconsequential to our Kingdom impact, giving us real cause for celebration.

As God's search-and-rescue workers in the marketplace, we must learn how to become righteously strategic and discerning so that we can lead the blind out of darkness, as well as thrive among unbelievers. We are called to be watchmen on the wall, vessels of honor and channels of God's blessings wherever we are planted. Our attitude toward our assignments should emphasize the reality that we are not our own. God is ordering our circumstances so that we might fulfill His purposes. We are on display for the Kingdom, with our highest vocation to bring God glory. Our fight is not against our boss or the competition, but against spiritual wickedness in high places. Our call is to stand against the enemy.

> **Missionaries in the marketplace are called to the Great Commission at work.**

Our "stand" against the enemy will require that we maintain a readiness to proclaim the Gospel of Jesus Christ. It will also require that we are ready to present biblical perspectives on the issues our co-workers face each day. With "love," "humility" and "honesty" as our calling cards, we will successfully deliver a message of hope, wholeness and deliverance to the spiritually destitute.

173

As missionaries in the marketplace, we must accept our Kingdom assignment to live out our faith on the job. We must know our purpose and understand that we have something of eternal value to offer. We are called to lead men and women to Jesus Christ, to disciple them and to teach them how to become successful in a manner that pleases God. We must work as hard as if Jesus Himself were our boss—which He is! In all of these things, we are charged to walk in integrity and exemplify His standards. Then and only then can we be the salt and light Jesus commands us to be. Then and only then can we influence and win others to the Kingdom.

Now it is time for a reality check that will help you apply the information you have read in this book. After completing the Marketplace Experience Self-Evaluation at the end of this chapter, write down at least two additional things you plan to do that will help you take Jesus to work and live out your faith on the job. Tape this list of things on your mirror, make a copy for your refrigerator and place a copy in your Bible. Pray that God will give you practical steps toward carrying out your list so that you can become the marketplace search-and-rescue worker He has called you to be. Meditate on whatever steps God shows you and decide in your heart to take them. Pray daily using the prayers in this book or other prayers that the Holy Spirit brings to your mind. Read and memorize some of the Scriptures we have discussed that line up with the transformation needed in your life.

While your list might seem a little intimidating at first, if you are truly yielded to the guidance and direction of Jesus, you will not be the one performing the work anyway. Through your relationship with God, His supernatural power will show itself in your life and work. After all, God is the potter and we are the clay. If you believe this, trust God and move out into your purpose and destiny. I would like to close this book by commissioning you in prayer for your marketplace assignment:

Equipping Prayer

Amazing Father, I thank You for unfolding Your Word and for allowing Your people who have read these pages to be fruitful in the marketplace. Grant each reader the boldness and courage to contend for the Kingdom and to convincingly live out his or her Christian testimony on the job. Help each reader to be the salt and light—the person whom unbelievers, as well as Christians, will run to when they want answers and aid.

Father, please help us all be purposeful about our assignments, ever ready to respond to Your leading. Commission us as privates, lieutenants, captains, colonels and generals in power and authority in Your name. Thank You for doing these things. In the name of Jesus I pray, Amen.

Marketplace Memory Scripture

Therefore, since we are surrounded by such a great cloud of witnesses, let us throw off everything that hinders and the sin that so easily entangles, and let us run with perseverance the race marked out for us. Let us fix our eyes on Jesus, the author and perfecter of our faith, who for the joy set before him endured the cross, scorning its shame, and sat down at the right hand of the throne of God. Consider him who endured such opposition from sinful men, so that you will not grow weary and lose heart.

Hebrews 12:1–3

Marketplace Experience Self-Evaluation

Record one attitude that might hinder your ability to "endure to the end" in the marketplace.

Based on the teaching in chapter 10, list one biblical principle you could have applied to your situation.

What steps will you take to excel in your current marketplace assignment for the Kingdom or prepare for your next assignment?

What are you going to do to "endure to the end?"

Based on the teaching in chapter 10, rate your new skill level at taking Jesus to work and living out your faith on the job:

    ____ 1.   A Little Better Prepared
    ____ 2.   Much Better Prepared
    ____ 3.   Equipped

Note: *To increase your skill level after your initial reading of the chapter, please pray for wisdom according to James 1:5 and read the chapter again.*

End Notes

Excerpt on page 72 was taken from *My Utmost for His Highest* by Oswald Chambers, © 1935 by Dodd Mead & Co., renewed © 1963 by the Oswald Chambers Publications Assn., Ltd. Used by permission of Discovery House Publishers, Grand Rapids, MI. All rights reserved.

Excerpt on pages 73–74 was reprinted from *The Pursuit of God* by A. W. Tozer, copyright © 1982, 1993 by Zur Ltd. Used by permission of WingSpread Publishers, a division of Zur Ltd., 800.884.4571.

Excerpt on page 90 was taken from *Authority and Submission* by Watchman Nee, copyright © 1998 by Living Stream Ministry. Used by permission of Living Stream Ministry, Anaheim, CA.

Excerpt on page 157 was taken from *The Heart of Praise* by Jack W. Hayford, copyright © 2005 by Regal Books. Used by permission of Regal Books, Ventura, CA.

Index

Dr. Vera R. Jackson is a marketplace Christian. An accomplished executive and university professor, she currently serves as president and CEO of a nonprofit organization and the senior leader of a consultancy.

She has authored and edited numerous articles and books. At conferences and workshops, she speaks frequently on the topics of taking a biblical approach to marketplace success, leadership, stewardship, family and work relationships and personal growth.

Dr. Jackson received her doctorate and masters in social work degrees from Howard University and a Bachelor of Arts degree from Trinity University. She and her loving husband, Wilbert, reside in Maryland.

To inquire about Dr. Vera Jackson speaking or ministering at your event, please contact:

Vera Jackson and Associates

vjackson@verajacksonassoc.com

www.verajacksonassoc.com

CPSIA information can be obtained at www.ICGtesting.com
Printed in the USA
BVOW02s1221050916

460698BV00001B/3/P